Weeping Kings and Wild Boars

Moments of Magic and Sorrow in
Forty Years Trying to Save the World

Jerry Eckert

ISBN: 978-0-9961710-3-8

Cover Design by Carmen Ruyle Hardy
Cover image courtesy of the Eckert Family

Printed in the United States of America
First Printing, 2016

Hot Chocolate Press
Fort Collins, Colorado

http://HotChocolatePress.com

A boutique publishing house based in Colorado creating books to warm
your heart, nourish your soul and spark your sense of adventure.

Become part of the Hot Chocolate Press Family:
- Like us on Facebook
- Follow us on Instagram: HotChocolatePress
- Sign up for our monthly newsletter filled with articles, recipes,
  stories and other things to warm your heart, nourish your soul
  and spark your sense of adventure.

Introduction

I struggled to write this introduction. How do you introduce to a book like this? Do you share some poignant anecdote? No, the book contains so many of them, humorous, insightful, and, yes, poignant. Whatever I could contribute would not add much to the narrative. No, I decided, I don't want to introduce this book. I want to introduce you to the man who wrote it. That man, Jerry Eckert, was my father. All that happened to him, as he describes it in these pages, is part of a long family narrative passed down from my grandfather, to my father, and finally to me. It is the evolution of how one man absorbed early lessons in cultural curiosity as he followed his father at work, translated that curiosity into a more academic interest in improving the lives of the less fortunate, and finally raised a family that, each in their own way, has carried on his legacy.

My father was a very unique individual. He was a study of contrasts – a gregarious introvert, a brash poet, a professor and a farmer, a self-styled mountain man who counseled kings - but the common thread that ran through all aspects of his personality was a tremendous intellectual curiosity that propelled him in both his personal and professional life. He was curious about people, often stopping to chat up total strangers on matters both mundane and profound. He read voraciously, mostly nonfiction, as if ever on a journey to understand the world around him. He explored the world. His professional life took him to some of the most remote regions on the planet, deep in the Himalayas of Pakistan and the Maluti Mountains of Lesotho. The people and places he came to know through his work made a profound impression on him, as this book will testify. With age, his explorations were closer to home, but no less adventurous as he climbed above timberline in Colorado, or hiked the Arizona Trail. Growing up, he always taught us that 'bored' was a word to be expunged from our vocabulary – the world was too vast and fascinating for anyone ever to be bored....and especially not my father.

My dad was also a caring and attentive family man. Although this book documents many of his experiences while travelling, it was to his home that he felt most connected. As a little girl, I waited impatiently for him to return from his travels. He always brought me little mementos of the places he was visiting – his way of telling me he was thinking about me even when he was away. He always came to our soccer matches, our tennis tournaments, our track meets. He bought some land up in the Colorado Mountains when we were very young, and our family built a log cabin together – a project that occupied a large portion of our younger years, and to some extent never finished. He wrote beautiful poetry to his wife, using verse to express her importance in anchoring his life. He was very much the gravitational center of our family universe, bonding us to a core even as each child in turn struck out on his own.

In his later years, instead of relaxing into retirement he decided to launch a new career as a writer, and threw himself into the pursuit with the determination that permeated everything he did. It gave all of us a chance to reconnect with him over a shared history that he was recalling or idea he was exploring. And of course we are fortunate that his passion for telling stories has resulted in this incredible memoire.

So how do I write an introduction to his memoire that captures such a remarkable person in just a few words? In truth, I can't. I can only offer these small memories of my own which will inspire you to read on and learn more about the life of this remarkable person, Jerry Eckert...my dad.

~Erin Eckert

Acknowledgments

Custom among writers demands a tip of the hat to all those who made a particular book or writing career possible, so let me do that briefly here. Any facility I might have with words tracing to my parents and our literate household is discussed in the prologue below. If I could remember their names, I would thank a fourth grade British teacher of English at the American Community School in Paris and an eleventh grade American with a passion for grammar and the now lost art of diagramming sentences in Frankfurt American High School. Michigan State University offered a seminal course in Professional Writing for Graduate Students.

Thus prepared I left my studies to tackle the academic world, and found myself driven by the system to write in jargon heavy, passive sentences about esoterica and raise my output of refereed journal articles. It seemed so meaningless. I could do it and I did, even winning two best published article awards from my professional association. The year I didn't play the game, I was punished with a zero salary increment. I wanted my writing to influence policy in developing countries and the tone and language of academic articles won't get your average Prime Minister to sit up and take notice.

Thirty-five years later, after my travels were over, I sought to return to my first writing love, literary nonfiction. I found that the 300 yard trip from my Agricultural Economics department to the English department was like cultural space travel, from one universe to a wholly different one. Undergraduate students laughed at my $50 words in that first class. A literary journal editor told me I might be publishable if my submissions averaged less than 4.5 characters per word, which eliminates most words of three syllables or larger. But several folks reached out with friendship and counsel to give my new career the launch it needed.

Sue Doe taught that first undergraduate creative nonfiction workshop. I am forever indebted to her for saying that I might become a writer if I kept at it. John Calderazzo welcomed me into two graduate versions of his Creative Nonfiction Workshop filled with MFA supplicants and the level of discourse rose accordingly. Gerry Callahan let me into his Creative Science Writing course and my final paper won a modest national award. Matt Cooperman, in his course, Writing Nature, opened my eyes to how beautifully a poet can put nature into words.

Then there were the many friends and family who weren't paid anything to teach me stuff. Laura Pritchett, arguably northern Colorado's best writer, edited this manuscript and told me to quit studying and start submitting. Kerrie Flanagan, director of the Northern Colorado Writers group, kept my feet to the fire heading toward an agent-ready draft. As members of my critique group, Paul Miller, Jeana Burton, Kay Rios, Denise Fischer, Melinda Swenson, Karla Oceanak, Jean Hanson, Sara Hoffmeyer and Debby Thompson waded through a lot of poorly crafted drivel before they succeeded in beating some proper methods into me. Shane Bondi provided seminal inputs on several chapters as did my sister, Susan Eckert who was my first reader on much of this. Lastly, Betty Eckert, who was there for many of the stories in this book, tolerated my venture into this new career, and kept me from overstating or misrepresenting the facts. Whatever faults or deficiencies remain in this work are, of course, my own.

~Jerry

Part I: Prologue

Everybody Has Their Story

My first formative memory starts with a vividly painted ox cart grinding toward my father and me on a Costa Rican dirt road. I was seven. The back of the cart gaped open. The driver stood up front goading his oxen into a plodding gait with a long bamboo cane. Dad pitched me up into the cart, then scrambled in behind. The farmer glanced at his unexpected passengers with some surprise.

"Let's hear what this guy has to say," Dad said. "Everybody has their story. And besides, the people who know a country best are its farmers."

Down the road we lumbered at oxen speed, great wooden wheels crunching gravel. Multicolored chickens lay inert on the floor, tied by their legs into a bundle. By evening those chickens would have been bartered for goods the farmer needed, like cloth, or kerosene for cooking, something he couldn't produce at home. Dad worked at a research institute nearby and his job included talking to farmers. "Feeling the pulse of the countryside," he called it. Chatting in broken Spanish with an unshaven farmer about sugarcane, coffee, chickens, and whatever else; my dairy farmer Dad was in his element. Twenty-five years later, I also climbed up on market bound ox carts in Pakistan's Punjab, to talk to farmers about their new Mexican wheat varieties. I advised the highest levels of their government based on their answers and, in the process, completed my doctoral dissertation with their answers.

Over the years, Dad's curiosity reached across the spectrum, from plantation owners to *campesinos*, diplomats to dilettantes, hunters to hawkers, always asking how they were doing and what they thought. Often he took me along for the ride. From him, I learned how informative, how much sheer fun it was getting to know people from other points in the human mosaic. Especially if we got close enough to actually share in their lives, like riding an ox cart to market with a farmer and his chickens. From my father I learned that local languages were the turnstile through which I could enter these other worlds. Ultimately I studied six of them although not all with much luck. And from him, I learned the power of listening.

We took that ox cart ride in 1946 near the unhurried little town of Turrialba. Beyond our jungle, however, the world had plunged into a period of dramatic, unpredictable change. A new world order emerged from the social and political wreckage of World War II. Global sea changes swirled around us, but how these might steer my future lay well beyond my second grade imagination. The Cold War was ramping up. Churchill's famous "iron curtain" speech in March that year gave a stark image to the schism about to engulf us all. Competition and mortal threats between East and West defined world affairs until the Berlin Wall fell in 1989 and the Soviet Union collapsed in 1991. We were all trapped inside a polarized, fearful world.

The Marshall Plan, which rebuilt post-war Europe's infrastructure, spawned the idea that economic progress could be sped up by outside help and capital investment in the latest technologies. Europe's economies rebounded so dramatically that the pundits called it "the flowering of Europe." Japan achieved similar successes under General MacArthur's leadership. Everyone noticed. In his 1949 "Point Four" speech, Truman made foreign economic assistance a core American policy, asserting "We must embark on a bold new program for making the benefits of our scientific advances and industrial progress available for the improvement and growth of underdeveloped areas." Within months American universities asked for central roles and economic development became the academic adventure in which I invested my career.

As the West and the East rattled sabers, or rather ICBMs at each other, the lesser developed countries clumped together as nonaligned nations. For decades, the West and the Soviets used these nations as a proxy battleground. Our weapons were foreign assistance grants, loans, industrial and farm machinery, military hardware, and in America's case, field programs with thousands of men and women on the ground working for change. My zeal for helping the little guy made me, by default, a foot soldier in this grand dance.

At a more personal level, the Marshall Plan drew my father and our family overseas for two years in France. It was our third overseas assignment. By now, I rather liked living abroad. Strange foods, local friends, the prestige of being part of the embassy crowd, new languages and cultures seemed not so exotic any more, just the normal, even expected, flavoring of my young life. Later, in our fourth country, I graduated from high school in Frankfurt, worked summers on a German farm using only horse drawn equipment, hunted

3

reh buck and red deer stag, and studied for a year at the University of Bonn. By the end of all that, I was fluent in the language and calling Germany my second homeland, *meine zweite Heimat.*

By the time I got to college, I had spent nearly half my life following my folks into Mexico, Costa Rica, France and Germany. I was hooked. I didn't know it yet but I would spend 40 years in foreign assistance, either overseas or teaching development theory and practice on campus at Colorado State University. My own family and I lived 20 years abroad in Africa and Pakistan. Indirectly, the Marshall Plan had pulled me in, shaped my skills and directed my career.

But first there was the military. The looming presence of the draft shaped the lives of my generation's men. Vietnam festered just down the road, an unstoppable, out-of-control debacle that would consume our nation. I opted for ROTC, a risk minimizing choice, and stumbled into two years in Air Force intelligence, spying on the Soviets from Dayton Ohio. And, of course, a six month "vacation," in Saigon as the war ramped up in 1965. Vietnam was country number five for me. With some sarcasm, I call this my hired killer era although my job was not nearly that exciting. Aerial photo interpretation. Behind a desk in a headquarters complex. Billeted in the three-star Majestic Hotel on the waterfront in Saigon. I carried a weapon around town but only because the Viet Cong put a price on my head. Each night I sent messages to USAF pilots based in Thailand telling them where to fly and what to destroy when they got to target. This was all very interesting but brought no useful career skills. I was spinning my wheels waiting to get on with life.

4

While I was busy playing spy vs. spy, India faced yet another major famine. A Ford Foundation team predicted starvation and played a major role in bringing this crisis to the world's attention. They also mounted country teams in India and Pakistan to tackle the problem. By the time I got to graduate school, food grain self sufficiency was the watchword-du-jour among agricultural development economists in training.

Studying for a Masters Degree under Professor Bruce Johnston at Stanford had left me fascinated with Nigeria and its exotic agriculture, personally committed to doing my doctoral dissertation research there. So, Michigan State was really my only choice for a doctorate. MSU was the "factory" that turned out most of the internationally-directed agricultural economics doctorates and their large research program in Nigeria supported their students' research with field assignments. Eighteen months later, I was ready, course work done, All But Dissertation as they say, ticket to Nigeria in hand, when the American Ambassador's cable arrived: "DO NOT ARRIVE - REPEAT - DO NOT ARRIVE - EVACUATION IMMINENT." The Biafran War broke out on a Sunday in Enugu where, without that cable, I would have landed on Saturday, the day before. Over a million people died before it was over and my Nigerian dream evaporated that weekend. In a sense, I was all dressed up with no place to go.

Six months later fate intervened again. By sheer happenstance, Larry Witt, my PhD advisor, was at a cocktail party chatting with Ralph Smuckler, another professor, who had just become Ford Foundation's Representative to Pakistan. Ralph mentioned he needed an agricultural economist trainee and did Larry know anyone. Eighteen hours later, I accepted the job. For the next year or so, I would collect field data for my dissertation on Pakistan's agriculture while also being useful analyzing data as part of the in-county Ford Foundation team of agricultural advisors.

Pakistan became my sixth foreign country of long-term residence. Americans working abroad say that your first country is like your first love – you will never truly get over her. Pakistan was the first country that I chose, my first as a professional in my own right. I arrived on a one year contract with a young family, full of wide-eyed wonder and a zeal for agricultural change and feeding the poor. That one year stint grew into eight resident years– a prolonged love affair. I came to respect a moderate version of Islam, spent forty percent of my working days in the villages, acquired enough Urdu and Punjabi to pass pleasantries with farmers, raised my kids with lots of international flavoring in their lives, and so much more. Now I could claim a "third homeland."

In Pakistan, I researched and worked with five, ten and twenty acre farmers, men and women who farmed as had their forbears for centuries. No electricity, no power tools, no information on modern methods, their implements made of harvested wood and bits of scrap iron, their field work powered only by their hands, backs and a pair of bullocks. Theodore Schultz, born a South Dakota farm boy, later a professor at the University of Chicago, gave us all a fundamental idea. In one little book, *Transforming Traditional Agriculture*, he showed that despite their poverty, small farmers were shrewd economists, maximizing profits on their tiny farms, a few pennies at a time. Their resources of land, water, skills, money, market access, and new information, were scarce. My job and passion became helping these "limited resource farmers." After thousands of farmer interviews, and guided by this "penny capitalism" paradigm, I came to understand their behavior clearly and could design policies built around what they could and couldn't do. Pakistan's top agricultural leaders drew me into their inner circle for advice.

My wandering international odyssey crossed paths with a kaleidoscope of people, places and experiences; you might call it a long string of fortunate accidents. They built like a spiral staircase, each step rising from those before. Of course, responding to the unexpected rests on values and abilities learned at a very early age, mostly before age six. This focuses the question of who I am on my parents. Looking back, I think I chose mine very well.

My dad expanded our family's comfort zone to embrace the world. Every time we got on a ship or plane bound overseas, he called it "Another Grand Adventure." We all shared his zeal.

Our mother gave us language, literature and vocabulary, and a moral bedrock from the depression-era rural Ohio of her youth and the teachings of the 1878 Charity Chapel Church. One of her special gifts to her three children was regular Saturday trips to the public library. One final piece of our language immersion was Mom's insistence that we use the dictionary. Her favorite phrase seemed to be, ". . . and the rest is in the dictionary." As in, "Mom, what's an epiphany?" Which brought, "E-p-i-p- . . . and the rest is in the dictionary."

Facility with words, their roots, variations and borrowed bits, provides a microscope into other cultures. To know the formal and familiar voices, to drop a colloquial phrase or term correctly into a conversation, to express sorrow, joy, frustration, anger – even to swear in the vernacular – these are powerful tools in cross-cultural relationships. In many ways, vocabulary helped me slip inside the defenses that people sometimes hold against foreigners.

All of which often made me a trusted insider in social and professional situations abroad. In one country after another, I would arrive as the project agricultural economist or team leader and before I left I had been co-opted into advising the national leadership. Pakistan's Prime Minister had me drafting policy papers he handed out to cabinet or used in press conferences as though they were his own. In Lesotho, an honorary citizenship was discussed and I was nominated to be that country's Secretary of Agriculture. In white-led South Africa, they gave me an office in the Prime Minister's complex, where I worked with his top economic advisors to help them figure out how to unwind apartheid. And Nelson Mandela's African National Congress adopted my recommended policies to redistribute income and wealth as their own.

There is a cost to all this insiderness. Once, across a campfire a hundred miles from nowhere in Pakistan's Sind desert, George Schaller, the internationally renowned zoologist, told me that humans have limits to our emotive capacity. Most of us, he said, can sustain only one or two intense relationships at a time. I think the same is true with national or cultural affinities. To slip inside another culture deeply enough to be fully trusted by the insiders already there, one must cross an invisible boundary leaving behind parts of who you used to be. To earn the implicit trust of my South African or Lesotho friends, to be nominated for a cabinet level office or hired to help tear down apartheid, I had to prove I was on their side. Not just with lip service and pretense, but in beliefs, life style and commitment. The joy lies in our friendships and the deep sense of pride that flows from the progress we made together.

The cost is the rootlessness I feel back home. When someone asks, "Where are you from," I used to answer, "Home is a brown suitcase." Each time, my pride at being something of a global citizen was tinged with a hollow feeling. At home everywhere, yet really at home nowhere, I was always a little bit alone.

My story of challenges met and overcome, of small and larger contributions to the lurching progress of various nations was made possible only by many extraordinary colleagues, close friends and even an adversary or two. Some of them goaded me into action by making me angry, like Aftab who you will meet in a later chapter. Others held out a ray of hope that something better lay just around the corner. Some things my friends and I did just for the sheer fun of it, like an impromptu meeting in Namibia that designed an ethic for the new South Africa. Other times, all it took was an intangible threat of impending chaos and bloodshed that often kept me up writing at night.

In each case I found remarkable individuals, people with driving commitments to changing something important, and who trusted me enough to share their passions, and let me pursue their goals with them. Together, we were like a constellation of comets, each of us on our separate trajectories, yet our paths converging for a short time into something of beauty and meaning, before our individual journeys flung us apart again. My trajectory started on a jungle road in Costa Rica, tossed by my father into an ox cart where I could listen to a stranger. No one could have guessed back then where that path would lead, who I might befriend, or what we might do together. I have been singularly blessed with the friendship and trust of many. This book, while it is my memoir, is also filled with their stories.

Part II: Baptism in Pakistan

Ten Cents

In late summer of 1969 I flew into Peshawar on a mission. I wanted first-hand experience in the mysterious Northwest Frontier Province of Pakistan, called simply the NWFP. The literature paints an exotic picture of a people hardened by life in austere mountains, tested but never beaten in battle. The Pathans boast a unique culture and a recorded history dating back to Alexander the Great. Most villagers live in isolated mountain valleys, loyal only to their local khans, out of reach of Pakistan's government. Mentally and physically tough, aggressive yet hospitable, staunchly Muslim, individualistic, fiercely passionate about their code of honor. I admired them.

In my first job after graduate school, the Ford Foundation had hired me to join their agricultural advisory team in Pakistan. The transition was abrupt. In November 1967, I lived in a married student housing warren in East Lansing Michigan, helping Sue with two very young children, living on a food budget of $12 a week, and studying for the final classes of my doctoral program. By January 1968, we lived in a marble-floored, four bedroom, air-conditioned house with nine servants in Lahore and a business card that said Agricultural Policy Advisor to the Government of West Pakistan. I was not yet 29. My job was to design agricultural policy changes that might make farming more productive on the typical 5 to 25 acre holding.

My mandate covered all of West Pakistan, including the NWFP. Yet outsiders knew very little about agriculture in this remote place. The province ranged from arid plains at the edge of the Punjab, through fertile, irrigated, alluvial fans planted to orchards, corn and wheat, to high valleys with crops fed by frigid snow melt waters. Above it all, towered some of the highest mountains in the world. This rich ecological diversity could, I thought, be harnessed to create jobs and incomes for rural people. I needed an on-site assessment. This would be new territory for me – culturally, economically, agronomically.

Before poking around uninvited, I called the provincial Secretary of Agriculture. The "village telegraph" works well among Pathans. Word of a foreigner asking pointed questions of the tribesmen could spread quickly. Suspicions could rise, doors might close. I might even face some unpleasantries from the local constabulary. To my surprise, though we had never met, the Secretary volunteered to go along and interpret for me.

"It will be good for me to see my farm sector through a foreigner's eyes," he said. He seemed quite pleasant on the phone. I suspect he may have been motivated by something else: he could better keep track of what I was up to if he traveled with me.

We met at the Peshawar airport and headed straight for the villages. The Secretary, short and smiling, was dressed in a freshly pressed, traditional *shalwar kameez* and Pathan beret. He had insisted that we use his vehicle, a polished black

Land Rover with official plates, which I feared would intimidate farmers in the villages. I needn't have worried. A few miles later we were standing in a field of fruit trees and wheat, listening to an excited farmer brag about his crops. We also visited a prosperous orchard owner who insisted we taste his apricots right off the tree. He took this chance to complain to the Secretary about markets for his perishable products.

Driving up out of an irrigated valley, we found a farmer whose main crop was opium poppies. The Secretary ordered a stop, hailed the farmer over and insisted that he explain to "this American" the whole opium story. I listened, fascinated, for nearly an hour. This man farmed unirrigated land – a field of stones and gravelly-sand really, on a hillside too steep to be plowed. For him, opium was the perfect, maybe the only, crop. His poppies grew well on this poor soil with nothing but an occasional rain shower. They needed no weeding or plowing. Just sow them and wait until harvest. We climbed up to his field, sat on our haunches and watched as he showed us how to extract a reddish viscous gum from the poppy seed head. He slit tiny incisions using a scarifying knife made of used razor blades. Then we walked back down to his mud-walled hut where he showed us how to clean the gum and wrap bricks of it in banana leaves. Camel caravans coming though his village at night bought his raw product. I knew from the DEA agent in Islamabad that this opium traveled over the Hindu Kush mountains into Afghanistan, on to Iran for initial processing, then to clandestine labs in France for refinement into heroin, and finally to dealers and addicts in the United States.

My new farmer friend mentioned how his modest income, almost entirely from poppies, adequately met his family's needs. He explained to me, an agricultural economist, the economics of his choices. If his land had been irrigated, orchards might offer a net return of 400 rupees per acre. If he planted dryland maize *and* the rains came, he might expect Rs. 250 from dryland maize, but only if the rains were good. By contrast, half an acre of opium brought a net of Rs. 4,000, just about enough to sustain his family for a year. To him, the ethics of this crop were simple – on his few acres, it fed and clothed his family when no other crop could.

The Secretary steered us toward average farmers for most of our interviews, farmers whose answers might typify his province, and we formulated a few new program ideas. Toward evening I thought we should expand our net a bit and I asked him if we could talk to a really poor farmer. He found one right away. Off to one side, partly ostracized from the village, was a dirt-walled hovel with a window broken out and a collapsing compound wall. In what should have been an enclosed courtyard stood an ancient Neem tree, the kind that repels mosquitoes. Under that tree, watching some raggedly-dressed children at play, sat a gaunt man with missing teeth. His name was Lal Khan. At our approach, he shooed his children inside. He stood rooted in the dust, apprehension in his eyes. He had never imagined that a foreigner and a senior government officer would pull up to his little hut, black Land Rover, cloud of dust and all.

With his polished political skills, the Secretary soon had Lal Khan chatting volubly. After a few minutes, Lal Khan led us to his four acres of rainfed wheat, decrying the prohibitive cost of fertilizer and his wheat's pitiful yellowed color. Each plant had so few stems, with dry empty seed heads; we all could see that these fields would yield very little. He was worried. He told us that he would have to find supplemental work as a day laborer so he could buy the extra wheat his family needed next winter. But he was from a minority ethnic group, a refugee from India, and would find himself last in the queue for local jobs.

Then I noticed something else. There were no animals around his compound. He apparently had no milk buffalo, no goats or sheep, not even any chickens. I noted, once again, his skeletal appearance and that of his children, now peeking out from the front door. In a burst of inexperienced exuberance, I said to the Secretary, "Ask him when he last ate meat."

The Secretary looked at me and, in English, pleaded, "Please don't make me ask him that."

"But I want to know. How often does a really poor man eat meat?" I insisted.

To cushion the question, the Secretary laid out a meandering string of Pashto sentences leading circuitously to what I wanted to know. Once the question was framed, Lal Khan looked at the ground for a long moment, moved some dust around with the toe of his homemade sandal, and then answered, "*Eid al-Adha.*" At *Eid al-Adha*, an Islamic holy day, animals are sacrificed to commemorate Abraham's trial with his son, Issac. In Islam one-third of the meat is consumed by the family, one-third is given to friends and neighbors, and one-third to the poor. Lal Khan and his family had received some of this last portion from a wealthy family for whom he did odd jobs. By admitting to that meal, he was also admitting his desperate poverty.

But *Eid al-Adha* had been several months ago, I thought. Then he recalled another time when the village headman's daughter married and an ox and two sheep were slaughtered

19

for the communal feast. These two instances added up to the total of Lal Khan's red meat consumption during the preceding year. Both events brought the whole village together regardless of tribe or caste, and in both, meat was shared all around.

Pakistan is not a vegetarian country; meat is expected often unless poverty intervenes. This is especially true in the NWFP where a proper meal includes either chicken, curried or roasted, or the local favorite, mutton. In those days, Wednesdays and Thursdays were "meatless days" by law, in order to contain the national appetite and avoid pricy shortages.

I learned two lessons from Lal Khan that day. One, quite personal, was that some questions cut deeply enough that the pain caused by asking must be weighed against the value of the answer. With apologies to Lal Khan for his discomfort, the second lesson gave me insights into the depths of rural poverty that shaped my work on three continents for the rest of my career. I learned that in remote rural communities of less developed nations, a few folks may be so poor that they must rely on charity, on ceremonial gifts, if they are to eat red meat at all. Their protein must come from other sources. This meeting with Lal Khan also made me a passionate advocate of small flocks of chickens, which even the poorest families should be able to afford. The nutritional benefit of at least some animal protein in the diet can be crucial.

Once I moved to Africa, to Lesotho, where animal agriculture dominates the well-grassed uplands, I noticed that many households had a motley collection of various animals hanging around but few households owned enough of any one species to be raising them commercially. Why so many, and why such diversity? Extending Lal Khan's lessons suggested an answer. Lal Khan's meat consumption had suggested that there are socio-cultural values to livestock that can outweigh strict economics. In Lesotho, there appeared to be a "socially necessary" livestock herd. Self sufficiency in a social or cultural sense means a milk cow or buffalo supplying milk for the children, enough chickens to provide the household with two eggs a week and a chicken as an evening meal once a month, and enough sheep or goats to provide one or two animals a year for slaughter. One measure of truly degrading poverty, partly because the whole village can see, is not having even a goat to slaughter for ceremonies. Finally, in the non-Muslim world, a single sow often forms a household savings account, providing a stream of marketable shoats to meet monthly cash needs.

* * *

Many years later, preparing a lecture for my class at Colorado State University where I taught between overseas assignments, I found an important bit of data. During World War II, in response to food rationing, professor George Stigler published his classic "The Cost of Subsistence," in which he estimated the minimum cost of a diet that met all the nutritive requirements then known for health. Using 1939 prices, Stigler found that for an active man, that diet cost $39.93 per year.

Stigler's cost, only 10.9 cents a day, caught my attention. I had seen that number before. In the late 1960s, Pakistan bragged to the world of its 8 to 10 percent annual growth in per capita national income. Yet, as I looked around in

21

Pakistan's villages, the welfare of the people I worked with was going nowhere. In fact, as food prices rose, many families' real incomes shrank. Contrasting the affluent urban setting in which I lived with the mud-walled crumbling villages where I worked, led to a sharp awareness of growing income inequality and its crushing burden on the poor. This impending crisis blighted Pakistan's future and, therefore, I thought, should be a major policy issue. To make this point for Pakistan's leaders, I did some careful calculations. My data showed that the poorest 40 percent of Pakistanis lived on an average income equal to 10 U.S. cents a day. I had not yet read Stigler's paper. But I wondered just how a human being could keep going, much less stay reasonably healthy on 10 cents per day? Most of their daily protein must come from cheaper plant sources.

Stigler's least cost annual diet included no meat, only the following:

Wheat flour	370 lbs
Evaporated milk	57 cans
Cabbage	111 lbs
Spinach	23 lbs
Dried beans	285 lbs

In these numbers, I recognized Lal Khan and the rest of the poorest forty percent in Pakistan. They eat about a pound a day of ground whole wheat in the form of *chapattis* or *roti*, their round flat bread. These chapattis serve as eating utensils to scoop up curries made, in poorer households, of spinach, cabbage, potatoes or even wild vegetables but almost never meat. Various legumes form their staple protein supply, the peas, beans, lentils, chickpeas, and others that are well known in Indian and Pakistani cuisine. Finally, I came to understand

22

the importance of the water buffalo; one or two per household, treated as pets, tethered to the front porch and taken to the irrigation ditch for a bath by young children every afternoon. Buffalo are the village equivalent of "57 cans of evaporated milk," on the hoof.

Along with millions of the very poor, Lal Khan and George Stigler both discovered the margin of nutritional subsistence. One came to the truth through applied mathematics, the other through centuries of adaptation and the raw struggle to survive. The answers they found are nearly identical.

While my visit probably did not help Lal Khan much, his candid answers to a foreigner's invasive questions enriched my understanding of village dynamics and of life among the poor. When I reached Africa in later years, I understood much of what I saw without having to ask those questions again.

But he gave me more than just professional knowledge. The sight of him standing there, all skin-draped bones and frayed cloth, trying to be helpful, with his kids watching from inside their hut, remains with me, as vivid today as it was then. Although I had already lived many years in five different countries, only Pakistan brought me, for the first time, face to face with the human side of poverty.

As we walked back to the Land Rover, the Secretary of Agriculture for the Northwest Frontier Province turned to me quietly, so he could not be overheard:

"Thank you. I never fully knew what that kind of life could be like."

"Me neither," I replied.

On the way to the airport we designed a small-scale poultry initiative that might add a few eggs a week and a chicken or two every month to the diet of the very poor. He promised to put this program high on the priority list for next year's budget, enlist the university to research the best breeds and feeds, and direct the extension service to train farmers in small flock poultry husbandry. It was his suggestion to offer small subsidies for the least advantaged so that people like Lal Khan could buy a start up flock.

Ismail

Ismail was angry. Panicked too. A small drift of wild hogs had visited his wheat field the night before, and when they finished, little was left. That morning, I found Ismail standing there, his feet green with the pulp of flattened, broken wheat. Shredded stems pitched about in disarray like green pick-up-sticks. Ismail alternately shouted curses at the nearby thickets and whispered fervent supplications up toward Allah. He had good reason. His family's annual food supply lay rotting at his feet.

I first met Ismail while surveying Pakistani farmers who were testing new varieties of wheat from Mexico. He lived in Muhajirabad, a mud-walled village at the bottom of the Punjab's social and economic scale. Refugees fleeing India at Partition in 1947 had settled here. They arrived with nothing, built their village on land not good enough to have been claimed by others, and were still dirt poor when I came across them some twenty years later. Among the most destitute, Ismail, formerly an "untouchable" in the Indian caste system, had converted to Christianity to escape that stigma. At least in Muslim Pakistan, he was allowed a small land holding, although his plot lay at the very end of a leaky village irrigation ditch making his water supply tenuous, his soil sandy, and his crop yields poor.

Ismail grew winter wheat on most of his five acres; his paltry harvest almost fed his family. He also gathered wood and cow dung in the river bottoms for his wife, who fired up a communal oven each evening, baking flat bread *roti* for several client households. I'd been in Pakistan a couple of years now and recognized that this family typified Pakistan's rural poverty. *Roti* made from Ismail's wheat along with curried potato or vegetables made up their meals most of the year, twice a day if they were lucky. Meat appeared on their diet only once or twice a year, when someone else killed a sheep or a bullock for some village festival. No one in his house had ever attended school nor seen a doctor in many years. Corncobs heated one room of their mud-walled hovel in winter.

I had taken Ismail some new, high-yielding Mexican wheat for him to plant. While he tested these seeds in his fields, I quietly studied him and his abilities. Could someone with poor land, few resources, no education and little training find, in this new variety, a chance for a better life? Would these seeds work on a farm as challenged as Ismail's?

Early results looked promising. His wheat sprouted abundantly and grew thick and lush even without fertilizer. I expected this harvest to surpass any he had ever imagined. I drove down for one last pre-harvest visit when his wheat hit the soft dough stage, grains swollen with a milky carbohydrate paste that would harden into dried, mature kernels in a couple of weeks.

* * *

The Indus and its tributaries, rivers that give the Punjab (*panj ab*, or "five waters") its name, transect the land in broad swaths, ribbons of muddy water and flood plain. Irrigation demands to feed Pakistan's millions claim much of these once surging rivers. Sand flats surround the water now. The river's former flood plain lies dry, half choked with mats of weeds, tall bunch grass hummocks, reed thickets and thorny mesquite. Few shade trees remain, the larger ones felled by fuel wood gatherers from nearby villages. This land of five waters provides a perfect habitat for wild hogs.

Sus scrofa, the Eurasian wild boar, thrives here. They eat well and their former predators, the tiger and wolf, are extinct in Pakistan. Jackals and village dogs give them a wide berth. These beasts of the river bottoms grow fat and fearless, secluded in their flood plain scrub or in dense stands of farmer's sugarcane, feeding on food crops that are badly needed by local villagers. That poses a problem. Wheat makes up half of these pigs' diet, sugarcane another ten percent. Each year, food crops worth millions of dollars are lost to wild hogs. Grudgingly, farmers must spend hours, often well after dark, trying to chase wild pigs from their fields.

Unfortunately, wild boar relish wheat in its soft dough stage. As the last farm on the ditch, Ismail's acreage lay at the edge of riverine thickets, on the margin between habitat types, where a rich diversity of food and cover allow wildlife to prosper. It had been a short walk for the pigs from their beds to their dinner, and they had visited more than once. Ismail tried to scare them off one night, but a big boar rattled its tusks at him in the moonlight from a distance of less than 30 feet, and Ismail hurried to the safety of his mud-walled house.

As Muslims, Pakistanis abhor wild hogs. Considered unclean, untouchable and inedible by Islam, the pigs are largely left alone. And with practical reason as well. Large adult males, some three feet high at the shoulder, can weigh 250 pounds or more. A cornered boar or a sow with dappled piglets at her feet can be dangerous.

* * *

After examining the remnants of his wheat crop that morning, Ismail led me to his mud-walled home. We sat in his courtyard on rope beds. His two ragged children, aged 6 and 4, about the same age as mine, peeked at us from inside a darkened doorway. The eldest, a girl, watched this stranger with curiosity. Her little brother hid behind her. I waved at them. They giggled.

"Tea" was served in coarse earthen mugs fired by the local potter. Poverty precluded serving real tea, which he would have had to buy. But his wife, the village baker, knew the right wild bushes whose leaves made a tolerable substitute, and not offering tea to a visitor, especially one "from overseas," was inexcusable. Our conversation centered on wheat and wild pigs, of course. He asked if some of my friends and I could hunt these awful beasts, these Devil's spawn, which had ruined his crop and left him desperate.

We arrived that weekend, a couple of hours before dusk – two friends and I, impromptu hog hunters with day jobs as diplomats. Armed with borrowed shotguns, buckshot shells and a few rifled 12-gauge slugs, we were ready to do battle. Ismail served us his special tea and *roti* with a boiled egg each. I noticed that he did not eat an egg himself. Those three that he served us may have been a week's supply of animal protein for his family. He then led us into the river bottom thickets below his wheat fields. We spread out, found our stands and settled into the gathering gloom. Afternoon's light faded. A gibbous moon, already risen, would soon replace the setting sun. River sands held remnants of the day's last heat. A breeze coursed through the flood plain, tickling reeds and grasses into gentle motion. Their shadows danced.

I picked a large hummock of pampas grass and climbed into its middle. This gave me a higher vantage point and hid me among the tall grass stems. I stood there motionless, just listening to the sounds of the village repairing to an evening's rest. Behind those mud walls, somebody's dog welcomed him home with a soft bark. Two little boys talked quietly as they led their family's milk buffalo home from where it grazed. Somewhere a one-lunged diesel motor punched the stillness, announcing that wheat was being ground for evening *roti*. Shrouds of gray and black eased across the river bottom.

Suddenly it appeared, seemingly arisen from the sand at its feet, under a mesquite some 30 yards away. A wild boar, rock gray and nearly motionless, surveyed its bit of wilderness with little jerks of its head from side to side. Big? I was not sure, for the shadows were playing tricks. But it was not small. Later its tracks would measure nearly three inches long, enough to hold a body of 200 pounds or more. Without so much as a grunt, he walked directly toward me and my hummock. He closed the distance in seconds, and then paused, stock still, ten feet away, perhaps sensing that something wasn't right.

I still see him standing there, both of us frozen, locked together in our moonlit moment. I still feel the breeze, warmed in its journey along the sands. I see the shadows dance. I think I see his razor tusk glint faintly.

For Ismail and his wheat, for his family's sustenance, for bragging rights among my friends, I wish that I had shot that boar. A 12-gauge slug from ten feet away would have solved much of Ismail's future wheat loss problems. But it was a borrowed gun, and in the dark I couldn't find the safety. I squeezed that trigger until it should have bent. It held. I cursed. And the boar evaporated. Two jumps, some flying sand, and a reed thicket swallowed it whole. The reeds stilled and silence followed, broken only by my pounding heart.

There it ended. Ismail still had his boar problem. And as a hunter, I had failed. Later that night we warmed ourselves around a corncob fire's glow in Ismail's mud home. Wild tea appeared. Ismail prepared a hookah as we talked. Knowing I would have to try this offering at least once, I watched as he held a candle to a small dung cake until an ember glowed. He placed it with tongs into the bottom of the hookah bowl. On top he packed coarse tobacco, and then he topped it with unrefined cane sugar. This was no ordinary pipe but a concoction of toasted, not burned, tobacco with a sweet aroma and taste. The pipe was swung my way first as a sign of honor. Hookah protocol requires wrapping the hand around the pipe stem extending the path of the smoke and then placing the lips only on one's own hand. I demonstrated for the other Americans there while Ismail nodded approval. The pipe rotated from one to the other. We all sucked tentatively. Like a good glass of wine in a quiet bistro, the hookah brought out an openness among us. We talked more or less as friends, not foreign experts and village client. We swore an oath – that, *Insha'Allah*, that boar would die another day, although I doubt it did, at least not at the hand of man. We talked of the rain, his soil, new seeds, a different future.

Because of their similar ages, we talked of our hopes for our young children. We couldn't know their futures then, but my son Scott would someday earn a pricey MBA, become one of the founders of on-line commerce, see his portrait on a wall of honor at the Smithsonian Institution, and then emerge as CEO of a succession of global firms. Ismail's son would likely farm five or six acres of scrubby land, work unskilled construction jobs in the off season to make ends meet, grow a few opium poppies and memorize much of the Qur'an. When poverty ground him into despair, as it sometimes would, he would numb his crying stomach with a tiny wad of opium gum and pray that Allah might provide for those he loved. If he were not strong, his desperation might also turn him toward violence.

My daughter Erin would take her doctorate in epidemiology into Africa where, with her fluency in French and Arabic, she would build public health systems in a dozen nations blighted by malaria, tuberculosis, and HIV/AIDS. Ismail's daughter might complete primary school, though probably not. She would likely marry at fourteen to someone chosen for her from a family as poor as her own. She would probably bake *roti* for village clients like her mother and would die before her fortieth birthday, her body drained of life by constant pregnancies, nursing, backbreaking work and malnutrition.

That night, however, we couldn't know their futures, so we talked in generalities. The corn cob embers warmed us both, their oranges dappled with a dance of blue and grey. Mellowed by that heat, we met, Ismail and I, in a place where our different histories were laid aside, where what remained was the fatherhood we shared. There we found a common cause: our hopes that our children might prosper, that their lives would have more opportunities than had our own. And that when they looked back from their own twilights, they would find that they had sometimes been happy, and had occasionally found times of grace, moments of intense pride. That night we also shared in one more thing. We had both seen moonlight reflected off the ivory tusk of one very impressive wild boar.

Evening Hymn

As evening descended on Islamabad, I often stood outside waiting for the cook to announce dinner, and with cigarette or drink in hand, just listened. A wild sound would reach out from the gathering night, snatch at my senses, carry them back into the dusk, and leave me changed. *Canis aureus*, the golden jackal, had spoken. Most of us living in that city knew them only as shadows flitting through the evening brush, or yellow eyes caught in headlights, scavengers gleaning carrion and garbage from the alleyways of civilization. These furtive little dogs suggested the "ghoulies and ghosties and long-leggedy beasties and things that go bump in the night" from which the Scots pray for deliverance. As I listened, they seemed to be singing.

Like the American coyote, jackals adapt well to urban life. Around humans, they live nocturnally. Cities and towns in poor nations provide ample refuse for scavenging, and jackals wax fat and numerous among them. In North Africa, the Middle East and South Asia, that "bump in the night" is probably your trash can lid dislodged by a twenty-pound beastie with gray and gold fur. Away from town, jackals remain predators and omnivores; nearly half their diet is plant material. Nor are they fussy; they gladly eat carrion when they can find it. Ancient Egyptians found them in graveyards, possibly feeding at shallow earthen graves. To them, the jackal became Anubis, God of the Dead, trusted Guide of Spirits through the netherworld.

Jackals hunt alone or in pairs, rarely in larger groups. Each family unit needs its space, roughly a square mile in which to hunt, to reproduce, or just call home. Unique among wild canines, last year's litter remains part of the family as "helpers," assisting with raising this year's pups. Both members of a pair mark their territory with urine and share most other chores as well. They want other jackals to know where and how numerous they are.

In early evening, as the hunt begins, jackals vocalize. With barks, yips or howls, mewling sounds and growls, the jackal has several voices. Their coyote cousins speak with more than a dozen sounds, each with a well known meaning. Science has yet to translate the jackal voice, but they must be equally as articulate. I think that with their evening song they are, at one level, socializing, and at another, reminding their neighbors that they are still at home in their own little hunting preserve and that the neighbors can kindly stay out.

Islamabad sits on an alluvial plain descending gradually from the Himalayan foothills towards dryland wheat farms at the northern edge of Pakistan's Punjab province. Along the western edge of town, for several miles, stretch the Margalla Hills, dedicated as a national park and nature reserve. The boundary line is crisp. Margalla Road divides upscale neighborhoods of diplomats and senior civil servants from a nearly untouched desert scrub that rises 2000 feet and more within the first mile west of town. The park protects gray goral, barking deer, leopard, Rhesus macaques, pangolin and other oddities. The golden jackal is everywhere, its numbers especially high due to the cornucopia of supplemental garbage, rats and an occasional unfortunate house cat just across the road in town.

I thought my kids might like to meet these jackals face to face, a personalized wildlife experience on a crisp spring evening. Erin was seven, Scott was five. I picked up meat scraps and bones at the butchery on the way home from work one afternoon, grabbed my Arizona coyote call and the kids, and set out on our expedition just before dusk. Their little feet skipped with excitement as we crossed Margalla Road. One hundred yards into the brush we found the perfect spot, a clearing of maybe 75 feet across with a thick thorn bush clump on its downwind edge. Erin and Scott sprinkled the scraps around the clearing before we settled into the deepening shadow of our hide.

We sat there a couple of minutes, watching the sun begin to sink behind the ridge. Unseen birds rustled into their evening perch. Hopefully, I put the call to my lips and blew a raucous screech, loud then fading off in seemingly pained spasms. In Arizona, this was supposed to say "dying rabbit" to nearby coyotes or bobcats. Here on the South Asian Subcontinent, what it conveyed to critters was anybody's guess. Perhaps the death scream of rabbits is universal. We could only hope. Another call or two and then, all eyes and ears, we waited.

It didn't take long. In early evening, cooling mountain air flowed down off the hills, through our clearing, past the thorn bush under which we sat, and out onto the Punjab plains. We knew the little fellows were near; their scent got to us first, flowing through our hide, hugging the ground like a blanket. Sitting cross-legged in the desert, gravel scraping our ankles, acacia fronds brushing our necks, we dared not move. Who would see one first?

Then, an urgent whisper from one of the kids, body frozen, eyes pointing. "Dad. What's that?" A second small voice added, "There, Dad. By that bush. Look." Sure enough, here he came. A large male trotted right out into our clearing and, to our surprise, sat on his haunches – not 30 feet away. Unlike other wild dogs, jackals generally sit when not moving, eating or nursing. Maybe that's why the God Anubis is always depicted with an alert upright jackal's head, a seated profile. This one plopped down just like he owned the place, looked around alertly, still oblivious to those of us hiding under the bush. Seconds later, his mate arrived, a little smaller with a smoother coat, probably a young mate. She didn't sit. Instead she circled around the bait, sniffing for anything odd, closing in, looking it over. Satisfied, she gobbled down a piece, then a second. Later she would regurgitate these bits of water buffalo for her pups back in their hidden den somewhere.

We watched this tiny panorama, frozen in the shadows. We whispered observations. The darkness slowly swallowed our jackals. It was almost time for us to go when, off to the north, so far away we barely heard it, a yip penetrated the stillness. We held our breath. Another yip. And then a yip-howl. Joined almost immediately by a second stronger voice with yip-yip-howl – the Margalla evening hymn had begun.

Just before that first distant pair finished singing, a second pair chimed in. I may have heard a single voice as well, a little closer to the hills. Just before each song was done, another group or two took up the tune, nearer now and louder. Discordant notes to human ears, somehow their voices blended, an *a cappella* harmony in many parts, moving down along the base of the ridge. To our delighted ears, a rolling cacophony ensued, demented demons from another world, fifty Anubis incarnations, debating which would be our guide in the afterlife.

On it rushed toward us until the two dogs inside our clearing took up the song, surrounding us with the din of raucous laughter. Then the song moved away, pulled by its own momentum, leaving us to listen as it coursed on down a mile or two, fading finally into howls so faint we could hardly hear.

For long moments no one spoke. Then, over in the city, an imam began his call to evening prayer. His "Allahu Akbar" led into a robust singing chant, praising God and blanketing the city with a moment's reflection. In the dark, we headed home. As we walked the kids asked, "Why do jackals do that, Dad?" I tried to answer. I spoke of territories, of bonding once for life, of social interactions in the wild. I sensed, however, these were only partial answers. My voice trailed off.

I may never know the whole truth of the jackal's evening hymn. But Erin, Scott and I will know that for a short while, in a South Asian dusk, we were caught up, surrounded and swept over and away by something Dad could not quite explain. Maybe it is enough, maybe even it is better, to leave a mystery hanging there and know that for a moment we had been inside that mystery, riding on a jackal's voice through a wilderness night.

The Visit

The December sun sets early in Islamabad. In fading light, I throttled the Yamaha down, leaned into the turn up my driveway and coasted to a stop at my front door. It was warm for this time of year. I found the ride home from work tonight refreshing, languid. "Allahu Akbar," the call to evening prayer, rang out from a raspy loudspeaker wired to a minaret in the next block. Soft smoke hung low across town from evening cooking fires in tea stalls and kebab stands sprinkled through the vacant lots. Quietly, the foot traffic of household servants and construction workers headed home.

My night watchman appeared to collect the motorcycle for its nightly hosing down. In a turnabout of semantic deference I called him Khan Sahib. The bike wasn't dirty, but it gave him something useful to do. Other than killing cobras in the flower beds and chasing jackals away from the trash, a night watchman's life wasn't very exciting at my house. Khan Sahib bummed one of my "Amareeki" cigarettes and we lit our smokes together. He was a Pathan, a tribesman from a village deep in the Hindu Kush with a tradition of hardy militarism and faithful service. He always smiled at the ironic humor of me, the boss, calling him, the employee, Sahib or sir. While neither of us claimed Urdu as our mother tongue, we each knew enough to jaw a bit. Another week was over and a quiet Friday evening settled down. We watched the sun slide off to the west pulling its cloak of ember orange and purples after it. I waved at the sunset and, not knowing the word for beautiful, said,

"That's very OK."

"Yes, Sahib. Is very OK. Very warm too. Tonight very warm."

"Wait one minute. Your rupees in house."

"Very OK, Sahib.

'You go your village this weekend?"

"Yes Sahib. Baby sick. I go."

"OK. That's good. Very good."

Not a very deep conversation. But three of us lived alone at that house, my indoor servant, the watchman and I and we had become friends despite our broken sentences.

This day had been unremarkable. As agricultural economist on the CSU On-Farm Water Management Research team, I likely would have crunched some numbers or written up a page or two of research findings. I might have made some phone calls, maybe lunched with a friend at the Embassy cafeteria, or made final plans for next week's field trip to a remote village. I really don't remember. That workday was nothing if not ordinary.

* * *

Arriving home should have been a nonevent as well. My house in one of Islamabad's elite districts had four bedrooms, marble floors, and an air conditioner in every room. It was also painfully empty. Footsteps echoed from floor to wall and back. My wife, Sue, had decided after eleven years together that she wanted a divorce. She had taken our two children six months ago and flew off to her parents' home in Olympia, Washington, to work out the details. Besides, her father, a retired U.S. Army colonel, was gravely ill with lung cancer. She wanted to be with him and her mother during the trying times ahead. I was stuck in Islamabad with a year left on my contract.

Life without my children turned out to be dull and lonely. Long work days usually led to long nights of more research and writing at home. I rattled around in this big house attended to by Allah Bakhsh, my only indoor servant. Allah Bakhsh, "gift of God" in Urdu, was certainly a gift to me. The son of our children's nanny, I hired him as a sweeper when he was 17 and we lived in Lahore. His single mother needed the extra income, and he seemed a bright, likeable kid. He proved amazingly capable so I brought him up to Islamabad when I moved. Now, at 23, he had replaced all the other servants, doing the cleaning, laundry, sewing and home repairs, bossing the outside servants, answering the phone, making appointments and cooking two really good meals a day. We also gave each other someone to talk to. Now that I lived alone, he was indispensable.

Cigarettes finished, I let myself into the front hallway where something struck me as odd. Little clues at first, just hints, nothing specific. My mind automatically slid into fix-it mode. Note to self: Gotta replace a light bulb somewhere. It's too dark in here. Second note: Speak to Allah Bakhsh again about running the air conditioners when I am not home. This whole house doesn't need to be chilled down like this. It feels like it's about 45 degrees in here. Third note: The whole darned living room is dim. Maybe one of our three-phase power cables is down. Call maintenance Monday.

41

I started down the hall to mix a drink and see what Allah Bakhsh had cooking. But I stopped abruptly. Twenty feet away, Allah Bakhsh was making dinner, shuffling plates, peering into aluminum pots, sorting silverware – almost without sound. The noisy bustle of kitchen life had somehow been muted. Then I noticed that the kitchen, like the rest of the house, seemed half lit, as though seen through gray tinted glasses. It was clammy cold as well.

"Allah Bakhsh?" I asked, perplexed, maybe a little spooked.

He turned, smiling as he did every night and asked, "Sahib ready for dinner?"

His voice, now from 15 feet away, sounded as though it had come to me down a great stone hallway. Hollow. Faint. Far away.

"Allah Bakhsh. What's the problem with the lights? And why is it so cold in here?" Sahib was still in fix-it mode, though not so self-assured about it just now.

"No, Sahib. Lights fine. I not run air conditioners like you say. I not cold either. You OK?"

After a pause trying to put it all together, I said, "I can just barely hear you." I probably looked a little spooked. He shrugged, palms up, as if to say he hadn't a clue what I was talking about. I asked for a few minutes delay before dinner. Then reinforced with some Jim Beam on the rocks, I paced slowly around the house. In every room the light switch brought a gray dimness, a half light response. The bulbs all burned, but each room crouched there, crypt-like, in the penumbra of some shadow. My footsteps sounded muffled. I clicked my tongue just to check my hearing. It was fine. But normal evening neighborhood noises seemed abnormally absent. And the temperature. A damp cold crept along my skin, slid beneath my shirt. There, but not quite there. The air seemed heavy, immobile.

Maybe it was me. I hadn't eaten much at lunch and I probably drank too much coffee. Maybe with something in my belly it would go away. I ate my dinner and read the paper. Allah Bahksh came in, cleared the table and brought dessert, seemingly without footfalls. He walked without a sound – specter-like. Food and bourbon obviously hadn't helped. I needed something normal to break me out of this. People I knew. Familiar sounds. I fired up my freshly washed Yamaha dirt bike and headed for the American Club where some embassy colleagues would probably be, suffused in beer and country music.

On the bike, the night, the warm wind in my face, were tonics. Most Friday nights, the senior diplomats in Islamabad did their diplomacy quietly, dining and drinking sequestered in their walled compounds. The lower ranks and bachelors headed for the Club. Ordinary Pakistani working folk found their way to their mud huts in villages on the outskirts, leaving the streets empty. One long boulevard led to the Club with a series of speed bumps along the way. If I hit them at 50 mph, I could have little airborne moments after each one. So I did. The Club was warm and schmoozy, swaddled in lost-loves-and-pickups country music. I won a game of darts, then lost the next two. The Becks was ice cold like it was meant to be.

After a couple hours, having almost forgotten the ethereal scene at home, I headed back. But once inside that front door everything faded as before into half tones. Only this time, some understanding snuck in through the gloom. I grabbed a yellow tablet, the one on which I should have been

43

doing my research that night. I wrote down a description of my evening filled with half-tones. And then I wrote: "I can't shake it. Something is wrong, terribly wrong, somewhere, tonight. Somebody's dying. It must be Sue's dad." I signed and dated it at about 11:00 p.m. that Friday night. Then I slept on the floor in front of one of those little space heaters with the coiled wire that glows orange in the dark, warms the small of your naked back and keeps those things that go bump in the night at bay.

Monday came and I was called to the Embassy to collect a telegram from the States.

JERRY. SORRY TO TELL YOU. DAD DIED FRIDAY MORNING. THOUGHT YOU WOULD WANT TO KNOW. SUE

My mind raced with thoughts, questions. *Yes, Sue. I already knew. I definitely knew.*

Islamabad is 13 hours ahead of Olympia. Friday night for me was Friday morning in Olympia. As her Dad lay dying in Olympia, he was also there in Islamabad, at almost exactly the same time. I don't know why. Did he have a message? Did he want us to get back together? He knew that wasn't going to happen. He knew by then that the kids would live with me so was he asking that I take good care of his grandchildren? Maybe he was just saying goodbye and thanks for the good times he and I enjoyed. Whatever the reason, I will never forget my father-in-law's visit, from 10,000 miles away, during those final moments of his life.

I've claimed to have seen beyond the horizon before, with other people and other events. Few believe me when I tell these stories although to me, these were completely real events. But Sue's Dad proved without any doubt that there are ways of knowing that I cannot explain. And I have a page from a notepad to prove it. When I visited his grave in Arlington National Cemetery we talked about it, me and the white marble headstone there. I heard no answers then either, but he seemed at peace. The only thing left was my thought, "Thanks for the memories, Colonel."

Economics, Viewed from a Village

After all my formal education, the fancy universities, the name-brand professors, I finally learned what really matters economically by looking around me in Pakistan's villages. At first I was blinded by the novelty of what I saw, relics of ancient times that seemed like a living museum. Gradually, however, patterns and dynamics emerged that revealed a vibrant, system of links and dependencies between people, the foundations of a society I had never known.

One of my MSU professors, Glenn Johnson, used to say that he learned his economics during WWII as purser on a ship. He watched people spend their money, barter with cigarettes and favors, get into and out of debt. Scarcity, quality and bargaining power set prices. His ship was a microcosm of a small semi-urban economy.

In one important way, Glenn's experience and mine paralleled each other; the players in the micro-economies we looked at couldn't get very far away. My farmers weren't confined to ship, but they were confined to their village by poverty and a very primitive transport system. In the late 60s, roads into most Punjabi villages were nothing more than dirt ruts. Lumbering bullock-drawn wagons or bicycles carried people and goods to town, limiting most trips to a radius of about five miles. Even then, except for district centers, many hamlets were little more than a bus stop, a mosque, a few tea stalls and a cluster of mud-walled houses. Trips to a developed town or city were a rarity. Economic self-sufficiency happened within the village or not at all.

How does such a closed economy work? Imagine a typical farmer; let's call him Mohammad since many Pakistani Muslims carry the name of the Holy Prophet. Mohammad farms 12.5 acres of sandy-clay loam in central Punjab, using a single pair of bullocks for draft power. The British colonialists gave his great-grandfather 25 acres if only he would resettle, along with his family and farming skills, from a more densely populated area onto this newly irrigated land. Two generations later, his father divided this square of land between his two sons. It's not rich soil and it's been farmed for 75 years so it won't yield well without fertilizer which he doesn't understand and can't easily afford. He has little control over when his irrigation water arrives, a critical input in Punjab's heat. He also has never been trained on his various crops except what his father and his neighbors taught him. Academics called Mohammad a "limited resource" farmer and his low yields and scanty total production reflect that fact. He is also classified as "semi-subsistence." When I arrived in Pakistan in the 1960s, probably two-thirds of Pakistan's farmers fit both these labels.

Westerners find it hard to imagine Mohammad's farm/household management challenge because it has been over one hundred and fifty years since their farms and rural life were organized this way. Without access to vibrant, diverse markets, family labor becomes the main farm input and the household is the chief consumer of farm output. The two, household and farm, are managed as a tightly interwoven unit. If the family is to eat, they must produce food, or something they can trade for food. The staple in most

Pakistani diets is wheat, ground whole and cooked unleavened as flat bread called *roti* or *chapatti*. At traditional 1960s yield levels, the average semi-subsistence farmer needed 3.5 acres of wheat to feed his family. To avoid risk, Mohammad plants five acres just to be safe. Around the world, self-sufficiency in a staple crop, usually one of the cereals such as wheat, rice, or maize, or in cassava or potatoes, is the single most important goal of limited resource, semi-subsistence farms.

Mohammad must provide his own draft power for plowing or transport and his only option is a pair of reddish-tan Sahiwal bullocks. To feed them, he diverts an acre and a half away from wheat in winter to grow Egyptian clover and another acre, on which he might have grown a cash crop, to fodder in the summer. His bullocks serve several farm and household needs. At night he can tether them in a fallow field, where their urine and feces become home-grown fertilizer. He also might tether them on someone else's field and collect a rupee or two for the fertility provided. More often, his wife and daughters collect the wet manure, form it into patties, and slap them onto the house wall to dry leaving their hand prints on each cake. Dried dung cakes are a key source of cooking fuel.

Self-sufficient Mohammad keeps a water buffalo for the children's milk supply and for the yoghurt his wife makes to soften the fire in her curries. The kids treat it like a family pet, bathing it daily in the irrigation ditch. It lives tethered on the porch, but it still eats and thus diverts crop land directly into milk, and more dried dung cakes.

His family needs some cash for goods that he can't produce himself; salt, kerosene, basic medicines, a new scythe or sickle blade, a chain to hitch his bullocks to the plow. No one at village level can really be wholly self-sufficient. He has three options. In the off-season he can look for the odd unskilled job, perhaps paid by the day to work with a local road crew hammering rocks into gravel to use as road base. He must squeeze his part-time job in between time he spends tending his crops and animals.

Since the family needs a little cash every month, Mohammad must grow something non-perishable, something he can store and that his wife can take in small lots to market to exchange for necessities. Both of his choices are multiple use crops. Corn stores well if hung in the dung smoke near the ceiling of the house so the weevils can't get to it. His wife can manage 75-100 pounds of shelled grain on her head when she walks to town, grain she converts to spending money. In addition, the corn cobs provide heating or cooking fuel in winter.

Or, in Punjab, there's always cotton. Mohammad grows an ancient variety with a light brown fiber. Although its fiber yield is low, it's the color of traditional clothing and thus highly prized. His wife can haul a head load of cotton to town to exchange for her monthly purchases. Germans call cotton "Baumwolle," or tree wool. They must have been thinking of this variety since this cotton plant is more stick than fiber. Mohammad stores his cotton trees in a pile near his hut for winter fuel as well. Of course, boll weevils over-winter in this heap of farm trash, hiding there ready to attack the next year's crop when it begins to fruit.

It was cotton that first showed me the inner workings of the broader village economy including households that own no farm land but live indirectly from the land's output. I knew that besides converting fiber to cash on market day, Mohammad's wife takes bundles of cotton to the village weaver, who spins fibers into thread and weaves a few yards of homespun cloth for her.

I visited this man one day and found him sitting on the ground under a shade tree, making his hand loom slap and hum in a regular cadence. Since my Punjabi was rudimentary at best, we couldn't talk much. But we shared a smoke, he sucking on his hookah and me pulling on a cigarette I'd brought from town. I was studying his loom, marveling at how seamlessly the weft and warp became whole cloth when a much bigger picture began to emerge. He had built this loom himself from wood gathered locally, without metal or purchased parts, only his own hands, an axe, knives and a sanding stone. It had taken him days to get it just right but he never ventured out of the village. Everything he needed was right here. In the end he had a rustic work of art which to him was equipment enough to sustain a professional career. I also thought of the local tailor who, using a 50-year old, hand-powered sewing machine, creates clothes out of uncut cloth. For a splash of color he may include a few pennies worth of colored silk thread bought in town, or he might make his own dyes from wild plants and colored earth.

Thus the wheat Mohammad's family trades for finished items of clothing is almost entirely wage payments to the weaver and the tailor. Except for that ancient sewing machine, they are not paying for the services of machines, "capital" to an economist, nor do they buy anything from beyond the village, the economist's "imports." And the artisans serving Mohammad's family are as poor as he is. The weaver and the tailor's household spending, the next step in the economic cycle, or the economist's "multiplier," will mirror Mohammad's.

Similar stories can be told for other consumer goods and farm implements needed in Mohammad's home. A village potter makes his water jars, food storage vessels, plates and cups, collecting clays from a nearby deposit and throwing pieces on a foot-powered potter's wheel. He fires them in a hole in the ground with locally harvested wood or charcoal, and his end product is delivered without glaze, coloring or other commercial flourishes. His handmade potter's wheel is another fine piece of rustic art like the weaver's loom, without metal parts or other components brought in from outside. An itinerant tinker makes Mohammad's cookware using only muscle, skill and some hand tools to hammer a sheet of tin into a pot or kettle. The village carpenter uses only hand tools and local woods to make beds, maybe a chair or two, a table.

In many villages there may be a woman who operates a *tandoor*, the earthen oven fired with charcoal in which *roti* is cooked for her client housewives each evening. From each measure of flour brought to her oven, she keeps a small portion as her fee and so feeds her own family. If there is a body of water nearby, her husband is likely the village fisherman, selling his meager daily catch to local customers.

Mohammad's axe, knife and sickles are dull at the beginning of the agricultural year, so he talks to the blacksmith. For a promise of half a bag of wheat at harvest, his tools get sharpened, or for a whole bag, new ones are made, heated in a brick forge by charcoal produced in a crude mud oven in the next village.

In the average Punjabi village, there are other landless families without artisan skills and they are the extreme poor.

Mohammad hires them to cut and winnow his wheat, for which they get to keep one bag of grain out of twenty. It's one of his socially expected duties as a land owner. Most destitute of all, the village beggar brings his musical instrument to the front doors of larger farmers in the morning, his only offering being a song and wish for Allah's blessings. His pay – a scoop of coarse-ground whole wheat for his family.

These are the artisans, a caste system that has diversified local economies with handed-down skills for thousands of years. In Pakistan's Punjab in the 60s, a remote village of 200 households or more could sustain a full complement of artisan services. However, even then the artisans' livelihood was threatened by growing access to the cities, the efficiencies of mass production and cheap plastics. Today with Punjab blanketed by cheap transportation and electricity reaching every village, these skills are likely gone, remaining now only as vestigial memories of ancient times. But they remained in place long enough to let me study them first hand and to find an inner dynamic to local economies that they hadn't taught us in graduate school. Around this dynamic, I crafted strategies to reduce poverty and close income gaps.

* * *

What does all this mean to an economist? A side trip through some arcane theory will uncover a hidden partial solution to world poverty. An economist looks at multipliers, the ripple effects of individual economic choices.

Say that Mohammad, our typical farmer, makes some money in the off-season breaking rocks on a road gang and with this, decides to buy a new plow. The value of the plow, a new sale for the blacksmith's business, is the "direct multiplier" of this new spending pulse. But the blacksmith needs inputs to make a plow. Even if he cuts the wood himself, he likely needs a piece of steel for the plowshare tip, a couple of bolts, and some charcoal for his forge from a nearby charcoal business. The value of these inputs is an "indirect multiplier." Finally, the blacksmith and the vendors of steel and charcoal all make a little extra income, which they then spend. The mix of things they buy with this extra income is the "induced multiplier," also from the purchase of a plow. Understanding economic dynamics requires following the money flow to find where it pops up; in what industries, in which towns, regions or countries, and among which population groups. Of great interest to me is how much flows to the rural poor in the form of new jobs. But it's much more than just jobs. As I understand life, especially after that evening spent with Ismail after I failed to shoot his wild boar, jobs mean more than just income, they bring a role in life and a sense of pride, based on responsibilities well met – like feeding your family.

This process of making money from each other's spending continues, one cycle after another until it is brought to a stop by "leakages" which take money out of circulation. In theory, leakages include taxes, savings and imports. While Mohammad likely pays no income taxes, he will pay a land tax on each acre cultivated and a water tax on each acre irrigated. He won't put any money in a bank, but he might put a few rupees every now and then into a jar buried in the corner of his house. More often, their meager savings are stored on his wife's wrist, as gold or silver bangles. And sooner or later his household will buy items made from outside the village, the plow tip, laundry soap, salt, kerosene, axle grease, items that village artisans can't provide. These are imports to the local economy – and a leakage of money to the outside world. Jobs and wealth created by these purchases occur beyond the village and cannot help the local poor.

The economist puts these patterns into fancy language and concludes that "the spending of the poor tends to 1) multiply among the poor, 2) pay for goods and services that are very labor intensive, and 3) spreads in patterns that are more likely to stay in the local economy for a while before trickling off to industries and industrialists in the larger urban cities or abroad."

* * *

When not in the field, I lived with my family in Gulberg, the most upscale section of Lahore at that time. Like most expats, our life was plush, with our own complement of servants and artisans, nine in all, a marble-floored, air-conditioned, four-bedroom house, two cars, Montessori or international schools for the kids, and all the rest. At age 30, I felt very much like a latter day colonialist.

If nothing else, Pakistani society was feudal back then with almost unimaginable differences in wealth, power and status. Our social circle included industrialists, diplomats, senior civil servants and foreign assistance experts from the World Bank, the foundations and the State Department who jetted in, hovered a bit and then jetted on out, like migrating hummingbirds. From inside this setting, I could not help but notice the spending patterns of the Pakistani elite. They purchased the latest upscale items manufactured in capital intensive industries, where the labor content of goods was low and the few employees were highly skilled and relatively affluent – the "labor aristocracy" decried by Karl Marx. Plus their consumption mix was heavy on imports; either final goods like air conditioners or automobiles, or components like car parts or bolts of raw silk. Thus when the rich spent their money, they paid for the services of a lot of capital, increasing the incomes of already-wealthy capitalists. The small share of their spending that paid for wages went to high income workers, many of whom were employed outside of Pakistan. Thus their domestic multiplier was lower and what did stay within the country circulated among the middle, upper middle and elite classes.

Once I put the pieces together, the contrast in spending multipliers between rich and poor was dramatic, almost a slap in the face. How could development economists have missed this? Had our theories led us astray? It was only a small step from this finding to policy recommendations. To address their endemic poverty crisis, nations must get some initial incomes into the hands of the poor and then let the multipliers work their magic. Today this is a sine qua non of development practice. In the 1960s it was a novel idea.

* * *

The received wisdom when I was in graduate school was that growth, focused on industry, owned of course by capitalists, would "trickle down" to the poor because industrial growth needs an expanding work force. Eliminating joblessness and then forcing industries to bid up the wage rate would eliminate poverty, or so they said. Yet in Pakistan, where this theory was pontificated, the economy grew at world acclaimed rates while income inequality soared to obscene, politically destabilizing levels. Here was a case study of trickle-down dogma failing badly. Unfortunately it would be another decade before this theory began to be seriously questioned around the world and yet another before the fallacies of the theory were fully understood. Economists had to gather better data on the whole range of multipliers before the full picture became known.

All those years knocking around in rural Pakistan provided me a clear picture of most of the problem's structure as well as what needed to be done about it. The focus of policy and development stimuli needed a total reversal, toward the lower half of society instead of the upper ten percent, targeting micro- and small businesses instead of capital-intensive industry.

There was, however, one small problem. Although I felt certain of these truths, my conclusions rested on anecdotal information. Thirty percent of my eight years in-country had been spent in the villages, intently watching, asking tough questions, sharing smokes, and yet my data were still mostly anecdotal. Pakistan didn't have official statistics to support or refute my case. An Englishman, Malcomb Darling, had completed a superb study of Punjab's Muslim peasant and artisan economies in 1925. Since then, nothing. Essentially I couldn't prove my theorizing.

Without better data, all I had to offer Pakistan was to try directing attention toward rural employment. My limited resource farmers and their neighbors had at least one resource, their own labor. Yet there were so many of them, with so few skills, and so little productivity enhancing technologies that wages hovered just above starvation levels. To survive, they locked themselves into inflexible semi-subsistence farming and social systems, which kept them imprisoned by their own poverty.

Certainly there had to be ways to break out of this Gordian knot. I reasoned that the starting point lay in the rural job market. Raw data straight from the depths of the village poor seemed the only way to get the attention of the politicians and policy makers. Most of them had little or no personal knowledge of how village economies worked, nor how they might reach the poor. I needed the hard data that would result from such a study.

The Dustbin Telegraph

My frustration rose toward fever pitch. I'd just spent five years on Ford Foundation's agricultural advisory team in Pakistan as Agricultural Planning Advisor to the Government of West Pakistan. I had an office in the Planning and Development (P&D) Department, met regularly with the Minister and Secretary of Agriculture and spent lots of time in the villages. One of my informal roles was to keep my finger on the pulse of the farm sector and bring that ground truth to senior officers who were stuck with their office bureaucracies. I loved this job but now, sadly, the end seemed to be rushing at me. I planned to head home, find a university job and let the family live in the United States for a change. Erin was two and Scott only four months when we arrived. Five years later, they hardly knew their grandparents or what life in the U.S. was like. Their world was Lahore, Pakistan. And, in a sense, so was mine. This was the sixth foreign country in which I lived. I had never lived five consecutive years anywhere before Pakistan. Yet before I left I had one last possible contribution to this country and a growing sense of urgency to get it done.

My job sent me knocking around in some very small, remote Pakistani villages. I walked their mud-walled streets, carefully sidestepping open sewers oozing along trenches down the center. My farmer contacts offered tea in broken cups, patched with copper wire by the local potter. They showed me fields of struggling crops, pointing to wheat leaves curled by drought, yellowed from lack of nitrogen which they couldn't afford. Yet the survival hopes of their families clung to what might grow there. In humble courtyards I sat on rope beds under mosquito repellant Neem trees, and talked, or rather listened mostly, as folks from the bottom quarter of society described their lives. Some raised their voice and railed at government, believing it had failed them. A few stared at the ground, shamed by their helplessness. Many spoke with empty hopeless voices. Among them, I saw grinding rural poverty at its worst.

Perhaps I was slow weaving these hundreds of moments into whole cloth. But finally I felt I understood the root causes of rural poverty and that I had some solutions.

I couldn't understand why government seemed unaware of this crisis, blind to the prospect that this much poverty might bring social unrest. But stabilizing this government was not explicitly part of my job description. In retrospect, maybe it should have been.

What really bothered me was more visceral. Pakistan's rural poverty just seemed so overwhelming, so crushing to the families trapped in its iron vice. *There but for the Grace of God, go I*, I thought and was then immediately swept with a feeling of guilt. The guilt of the advantaged when faced with the plight of the less fortunate. Second cousin to survivor's guilt. I think this form of remorse drives a lot of us to careers in foreign assistance.

My guilt demanded action. If possible, I would place this issue, both its causes and solutions, on the front burner in national policy discussion. My village contacts with their open sewers and meatless diets, their uneducated children who would likely never see a doctor, their wives with life expectancies under 40 because of the drains of constant malnutrition, pregnancy and nursing, these folks needed their government to embrace a new development paradigm. I had to grab the attention of politicians and point them toward poverty. And that could only occur with an argument based on solid ground truth supported by real village data, the kind of numbers they couldn't ignore. Such data had never been collected so I designed a survey to spotlight rural poverty. Pakistan needed this new policy focus, it seemed to me, if it was to remain a stable nation capable of bringing better lives to its citizens. So, whether or not it was in my job description, I had to do this.

Ideally, the Planning and Development Department should run this study. My recent doctorate gave me all the tools I needed to analyze the data, and I probably had the writing skills to make the case for the rural poor persuasively. But we had no data. If P&D were to collect the numbers, they might be forced to believe the final results and then they just might act on them. P&D's active support was critical. Beyond someone simply saying they had no objection, I needed all the normal survey paraphernalia; Land Rovers, drivers, petrol, interviewers, field team leaders, a budget for meals, – in short a full-out effort mounted by the P&D. With only three months left in country, I needed it quickly.

But, it was not going well. In fact, it was not "going" at all. One obstacle after another arose. Each roadblock came from P&D's Chief Economist, on paper the very man I advised on agricultural policy. Let me call him Aftab. Aftab never really said No, but he never said Yes either. He just strung out the process interminably. He knew that in a few weeks I would be gone and out of his hair.

"I'd like to," he would say, "but our interview staff are in the field, busy with other jobs."

"Sorry. The department's vehicles are with the Honorable Minister all week," he said.

Or else, "I checked. Our budget for field research this year won't cover your survey."

As a result, orders to launch never materialized. If I had to, I could write the report after I got to the States, but not without the raw data, and my window before departure was closing. I believed that, if I could get it off the ground, this study might reshape Pakistan's future. My desperation mounted. I'd seen too many skinny kids to let it go.

* * *

I came here in 1968 partly because my Ph.D. advisor pointed out Pakistan's phenomenal GNP growth rate. At the time, I had been holding out, hoping for a place in Africa to do my dissertation research.

"Eight to ten percent per person per year." he said, noticeably excited. "Get over there. Get in on the ground floor. Learn how that country works. With a growth rate like that, development economists will soon hail this country as a major success."

The Ford Foundation then offered me the trainee position in Lahore on their agricultural team, a job which also promised a unique setting for my doctoral research. My wife, our two young children and I got on a plane and headed out. I was about to fall in love with this fascinating place. Before I left Pakistan for good, this one year tour would extend into eight resident years in country.

Within a month of arrival, my Ford Foundation boss sent me into the villages to find out why farmers failed to adopt chemical fertilizers to go with their new Mexican wheats. If they merely replaced the old varieties with these Mexican seeds, yields doubled. But, if they fertilized them well, yields quadrupled. Why, then, were farmers not buying fertilizers? This anomaly seemed just the problem for a neophyte agricultural economist, the newbie on the field team. Ford assigned a car and Abdul Ghafoor, a driver with great people skills who spoke five languages. Ghafoor would become my bridge into Punjabi villages and their people that made my dissertation research possible a couple years later. To him, I must have seemed like a kid in a candy store with all the questions I asked on that first trip.

The fertilizer answers were easy. Fertilizers came mostly from foreign assistance. Seven or eight donor nations provided 10-12 types of fertilizer, each differing in color, chemical content and packaging. Some compounds were totally useless on Pakistani soils. Most Punjabi farmers could neither read nor write. Yet donors, competing with each other for sales, bombarded farmers with enough conflicting sales pitches to confuse everyone. Since fertilizers cost money, even with donor subsidies, farmers simply backed away from these unfathomable foreign curiosities.

More remarkable to me, I found no one in Punjabi villages, at least not those I visited, who ever saw any of that reported 8-10 percent income growth. Could the World Bank be wrong? Nine percent annual growth will double anything in eight years. Yet, the people I met hadn't doubled their family incomes in a generation or longer. In fact, these villagers found that merely hanging on was a struggle, and getting ahead in life was a disappearing hope. I could sense their frustration, and imagine its violent results. That first village fertilizer use survey, my baptism into Third World reality, redirected my life. I had seen what it was like simply trying to live, much less grasp a small bit of dignity, on ten cents per person per day. Now I would attempt to do something about it.

As I dug deeper into Punjabi culture, I noticed no one ever really starved. A centuries-old social support network kept everyone afloat, if just barely.

Village economies and the people within them seemed tightly interwoven. I looked for points of leverage, nodes in the social web where an economic pulse received by a few would ripple out more widely, creating new incomes and opportunities for others. Looking deeper I uncovered patterns that we had not been taught in graduate school. If the poor had a little money, they likely bought goods or services from their neighbors and others who were equally poor. I reasoned that if new incomes could reach at least a few of the poor, that money would then circulate, reducing poverty more widely in the local area. My challenge was to document these pathways of money and patronage and build growth strategies around them. I didn't know it yet, but my career was about to veer off in a wholly new direction. For the next twenty years I would focus on rural labor, poverty and income inequality.

Aftab, however, seemed determined that this study would never take place. Every day or two, I pitched up in his office asking if the previous obstacle had been removed. Each time something new arose. Each time he smiled in his slightly patronizing way. It became obvious that no foreigner would ever achieve anything of merit on Aftab's turf.

My office mate at the time was Jiri Prazak, an economist who had fled Czechoslovakia, made his way to the U.S., got his green card and now worked for the United Nations Development Program. Jiri and Jerry, the two ex-pats advising the P&D Department, Government of West Pakistan. We shared an office full of clunky colonial furniture, an overhead fan, cheap metal ashtrays and a peon right outside the door who brought us essentials such as pins, paper, ink for the ink wells, and tea. Just holler at the door, in true colonial fashion, *Doh Chai Lao*, and with much clattering of chipped porcelain cups and metalware, two cups of thick black tea arrived. Milk was available but you had to spoon out the flies. He bowed slightly and called us *Sahib*, his existence justified.

One morning I vented my frustration on Jiri. I felt powerless. I couldn't bypass Aftab and go straight to the Director General without Aftab finding out and throwing me out on my ear. Getting fired now, just four weeks before departure, would embarrass a lot of people. Jiri was quiet for a moment. Then he offered a small story.

"Back in Czechoslovakia, the secret police would go through our waste baskets at night to see if our trash was subversive."

"Really?" I asked, surprise in my voice. I should have guessed, having once been in the intelligence game. But my "spying" took place from an air base in Dayton, Ohio, guessing at Russia's weapons capabilities using high-tech satellite intercepts, photographs of giant rockets parading through Red Square on May Day, and recorded heartbeats of Soviet cosmonauts in orbit. It had never occurred to me there could be intelligence value in something as mundane as office trash.

"Yes," he answered. "We sometimes sent messages to the top guys this way without going through all the tiny minds in the middle. We drafted notes that we wanted them to read and then dropped them in the dustbin. In the morning, they would know."

I sat pondering this new insight for a few minutes. Then I took a pad of yellow lined paper and scribbled out a letter to my Ford Foundation boss. The draft detailed the importance of the proposed survey, and then clearly itemized every blockage Aftab had thrown in the way. The letter closed with an apology. I was, I wrote, so close to being able to offer something unique, something really important, but now it seemed too late. Sadly, I must leave for home with the job unfinished.

This draft spread over three pages, hand written as if in a hurry, with scratch-outs, word changes, a note or two in the margin. It looked very much like a first draft. Then, after Jiri went home, I crumpled my draft into paper balls and threw them in the dustbin. I was out of options. If this didn't work, then the driving forces behind jobs and incomes for the rural poor would never be documented, at least not by me. My last big effort, the culmination of five years learning of, and loving village life, would fail.

That was Friday. I arrived at work on Monday to find the Director General's personal peon standing outside my door chatting with my guy. In the tone of an executive suggestion I was "invited" to come straight away to the DG's office, which contained even bigger clunky colonial furniture, the same cheap metal ashtrays and, rank hath its privileges, a real air conditioner. The DG was all smiles.

"*Chai Lao*," he sang out, and his man bustled off for tea, the good stuff, probably Earl Grey, with milk, without flies, served in fine china.

"Won't you have a seat, Dr. Eckert? Tell me how your rural labor survey is going."

Talk about cutting to the chase. I stood there, flabbergasted. Jiri had called it, spot on. They read through your trash, even here in Lahore, in an office as nonstrategic as a provincial P&D Department.

Since I had nothing to lose, I unloaded the whole sad tale on the DG. For about 20 minutes he listened and asked understanding questions. I got the sense that he already knew the answers. He then tapped his buzzer summoning his peon back into the room.

"Bring in the Major," he ordered.

In 30 seconds, a smartly dressed, middle-aged man with an erect bearing and a tightly clipped mustache joined us. He had been standing close by, waiting for this summons.

"This is Major Chaudhry of the Pakistan Army."

"Retired," corrected the Major. They were obviously friendly colleagues.

"Major Chaudhry will organize all the resources for your survey. He will also command the field workers. You two must work together so that this is a first class project. How soon can you start?" After three months of growing frustration, I sat there, stunned. Not only did the DG know my problem before I came to work that Monday, he had already solved it. Here sat a man who put Pakistan first, above any personal agendas. I wanted to salute, but it didn't seem right.

The Major and I went straight to my office, ordered more *chai*, and sat down to plot logistics. My tea guy appeared much more obsequious with the Major present. He even found some biscuits to go with the tea. When he got home that night, I'll bet he told his whole family about his big day.

Then I went home and worked through the night to define the survey, choose who should be interviewed, and frame the questions. Distinct questionnaires emerged for the five generic classes of village jobs; small, medium and large farmers, landless laborers and village artisans. Next morning, Ford Foundation mimeographed the hundreds of copies we needed in the field.

Major Chaudhry hit the highway with military precision at 0500 hours on Wednesday with three Land Rovers full of interviewers and a supply vehicle hauling enough food and bedding to survive the Sahara. I caught up with them twice a week in remote rest houses for progress reports and to handle questions that arose. They crisscrossed the Punjab, interviewing 200 villagers in two weeks. When the field work ended I had one week left in country.

Then the Director General pitched a curve. He insisted that the questionnaires be given to him personally. I thought Aftab might get his hands on them and lock them in some mildewed closet where hungry rodents would be the only beneficiaries. I badly wanted my own set for analysis. However, no one in 1971 Lahore had a photocopy machine. Switching to Plan B, Ford Foundation ran their mimeograph again for 200 more blank questionnaires. Then we reached back 100 years to a technology from Rudyard Kipling's era. We sent a driver into the bowels of old Lahore where scribes still sat cross-legged on the sidewalk offering their services as stenographers. The driver returned with five scribes, young men uncomfortable speaking English but able to copy English accurately. Manually they duplicated a second set of questionnaires in one six-hour day.

Not trusting the Pakistani post, nor Aftab's possible friends in the postal service, I carried the duplicates on the plane to the U.S. in my lap. Once in the United States, those surveys became raw data in computer files, and then central tendencies, standard deviations, trend lines, outliers and all the arcane things that delight economists. While I looked for a new job, I played with the numbers and scribbled out a text. Once Colorado State University hired me, they were kind enough to type and print the final report, "Rural Labor in Punjab: Analysis and Policy Implications."

Six months later Colorado State sent me back to Pakistan, family and all again, for a three-year assignment on their water management research team. The report went with me in the luggage and on arrival, I hand delivered the 200 copies to the Director General of P&D. He took them directly to the Governor of Punjab and to the provincial cabinet. I had finished my Ford Foundation job and now turned toward my new assignment.

A year later, to my surprise, Prime Minister Z. A. Bhutto's Special Assistant for Agriculture summoned me to Islamabad to lead a handpicked task force charged with writing a new rural employment strategy for Pakistan. They confined us to a high rise government office with sleeping quarters, fed us box lunches and told us we could come out when we produced a strategy that would pass Parliament's scrutiny. It took two days, but the National Cabinet did adopt our results as policy. Slowly the country was awakening to their poverty crisis or at least I thought so. Policies began to emerge using the labor market as part of the poverty solution. Fifteen years later, the keynote speaker at the International Agricultural Economics Association conference in New Delhi cited this Punjab rural labor study as the best of its kind ever done. I never did see Aftab again. I heard he was sent abroad "for additional training" and then took a high profile job with the World Bank.

All because of three crumpled pages of yellow tablet thrown into a colonial dustbin in Lahore in 1971.

* * *

Epilogue

Looking back from 40 years down the road, I am appalled and greatly saddened. Either Pakistan did not act soon enough or took action but without serious commitment. Or maybe they never really saw the poverty and inequality amongst them, nor sensed its explosive potential. Maybe my theory was wrong but I doubt it. Whatever the cause, Pakistan today, that country I once loved, is a developmental basket case, playing with nuclear weapons. It has evolved into a country in which political opponents are assassinated, ex-presidents executed for their crimes and the world's most hunted terrorist found shelter. The military and the Inter-Services Intelligence agency run the settled parts and the Taliban controls the rest. The sons and grandsons of my farmer friends carry AK-47s over their shoulders when plowing their fields or walking to market. And they probably still haven't doubled their family's incomes in any real sense. But all that is another story for another time.

Departing Pakistan

This would be my last visit to Faizalabad, a sprawling unkempt industrial city in the middle of Punjab. Eight years in Pakistan would soon end and the whole process of packing out, farewell parties and tying up loose ends at the office would begin in a couple of weeks. My time for field work had passed.

When I joined the Ford Foundation agricultural team, Pakistan was hungry. They imported 40 percent of their staple food grains, mostly on concessionary terms from the United States. A regional famine in Bihar, India in 1967 had catapulted food grain self sufficiency to the top of the development agenda for national programs and foreign donors alike. Norm Borlaug and the International Center for Maize and Wheat Improvement (CIMMYT) had an answer to South Asia's hunger – dwarf wheats. A simple idea, really, based on two genes found hiding in Japanese wheats by scientists on General MacArthur's occupation team in 1947. This novel idea, a new plant architecture, captured everyone's imagination; a wheat with lots of short thick stems rather than the few tall spindly tillers of earlier varieties. These dwarf wheats soaked up fertilizer, produced large seed heads laden with heavy grains and refused to fall over and rot. A Green Revolution was born. Borlaug would receive the 1970 Nobel Peace Prize for his dedication and lifetime of pioneering work.

71

His authorized biography is titled, "The Man Who Fed the World."

The Ford agricultural team in Pakistan worked in partnership with CIMMYT. Dr. Ignacio (Nacho) Narvaez Morales, from the central CIMMYT staff, lived in Lahore as part of the Ford team and led the in-country work on wheat. Nacho and Norm set up testing sites to see how varieties bred in Mexico would perform under local conditions. Their premier Pakistani site was the Ayub Agricultural Research Institute just outside of Faizalabad where they teamed up with Dr. S.A. Qureshi, Chief Cereal Botanist. It was a stellar team. In addition to Borlaug's much deserved award, Nacho earned international renown as the "Father of Dwarf Wheats." Dr. Qureshi won the Gold Medal for lifetime achievement from the Pakistan Academy of Sciences. I was privileged to work with Dr. Qureshi and his deputy, Noor Moh'd Chaudhry on fertilizer and irrigation trials. Together we won a national award for our research, which the newspaper headlined with "Their Work Will Feed Millions of Our People," the kind of results most change agents can only dream of.

CIMMYT's plan emphasized plant breeding to develop and test new varieties. Promising new strains were sent to collaborating researchers in several countries to be tested in local soils and climates. Funded and staffed largely by the Ford and Rockefeller Foundations, similar in-country adaptability testing could be found around the world with wheat and maize varieties from CIMMYT and rice from the International Rice Research Institute in the Philippines. In Pakistan, one dwarf wheat showed enormous promise, poised to sweep the country. They named it Mexipak.

I wanted my doctorate in agricultural economics, not cereal genetics. I wanted to know what Mexipak really meant for the livelihoods of small-scale farmers and their families. Could they manage these seeds with the resources and knowledge they had at hand? With what costs and profits? Could a five acre farm now feed its family with Mexipak when five acres of traditional wheats did not quite suffice? Ford decided my research should be official duty, gave me six months to finish the job and assigned the gifted multi-lingual Abdul Ghafoor as my driver-translator, my buddy in the boondocks. Criss-crossing the Punjab, we looked for people to interview, farmers who were cultivating the typical five to twenty irrigated acres and who also grew both Mexipak and a traditional variety. Two fields under the same farmer's care, growing in the same soil, plowed with the same bullocks, should, I reasoned, show the advantages Mexipak offered, if any.

In 1969-70, Mexipak was still something foreign, untrusted and seen as possibly risky by farmers living close to their margin of survival. Many smaller, subsistence farmers tested a few pounds of seed on a piece of unneeded land, their "playground," they called it, keeping their normal acreage planted to the old varieties so their family's food supply was not threatened. They also had poor information on how to grow this new crop. Farmers were confused and apprehensive. Whether translated from Punjabi, Urdu, or Gujrati, Ghafoor and I got an earful.

"I can't understand these chemical manures," they complained, referring to the fertilizer recommendations. "There is this white powder, the yellow powder, that white one that looks like shotgun pellets, and the red and tan one that looks like cherry pits. What must I do?"

"When must I plant this Mexi?" others wanted to know.

"How do I irrigate your Mexipak? My field isn't level and last year the Mexi all died on the high spots. Mexi is not happy without water."

My research clearly showed that dwarf wheats could out-yield traditional varieties 3 to 1 under the management of small farmers, but only with ample, properly applied water and fertilizer. Farmers told us in no uncertain terms that managing these inputs was tricky business. Breeding was not enough. They needed information on cultivation methods, planting dates, seed depths, seeding rates, irrigation timing and frequency, fertilizer quantities, time and method of application – the whole gamut. And they needed it tailored specifically to "Mexi." They would not find their answers from wheat research devoted almost entirely to cross-breeding and variety testing.

After turning my dissertation in at Michigan State, I returned to Pakistan with Colorado State University's water management research team in July 1972 with a job description that included irrigation research. Wheat, the crop that fed the nation, is a winter crop in Pakistan, planted in November. Plenty of time remained to plan a research program for the coming 1972-73 season. Maybe I could now answer some of those farmers' questions. What I planned was not agricultural economics, it was basic agronomy. Logically this research should have been planned by an agronomist. But the CSU agronomist would not arrive until too late for this season and, besides, I had learned the basics of wheat agronomy from the master, Nacho.

Off I went to talk up wheat experiments with scientists at the Ayub Agricultural Research Institute. There I found Noor Mohammad Chaudhry, Assistant Cereal Botanist under Qureshi, who had recently returned from a degree in the U.S. Noor shared my passion for agronomy, the science of growing crops. As a counter point to the breeding and variety testing program, we designed a limited set of experiments combining different irrigation and fertilizer treatments. Of course, in each test plot we used Mexipak.

That first year our inexperience produced a complete crop failure and a good laugh. The second year, however, we got it right and planted a full acre of trials. Results were excellent. The data promised several recommendations about how to fertilize and irrigate Mexipak. The third year we added irrigation timing, some plant physiology with a razor blade and a microscope, plant spacing trials and we included phosphorus in the fertilizer mix. Noor enthusiastically planted nearly five acres of agronomic trials, an area almost as large as the breeding plots. People started paying attention and Noor began to get some credit for this work. At my urging he took some of our most basic fertilizer tests off the research station onto farmers' fields to give them an acid test under village conditions. This novel approach to field testing became the first Pakistani application of what ultimately became the world wide practice of farming systems research.

It was at the end of this third year of trials that I visited Faizalabad for the last time. I came out here to tie up some loose ends with the agricultural economists at the University of Agriculture, after which we had tea. The department's faculty then walked out to the car with me.

"Khuda Hafiz" (May God be Your Guardian.) The chairman and I shook hands. "When will we see you back here?"

"Hopefully before too long." I paused at the car door. "You know I'm a Punjabi at heart"

"Insha Allah, before too long." They smiled at that thought but I knew it was unlikely.

It was a little after 4:00 p.m. We had about an hour before dark and the long drive back to Lahore – time for one last look at the wheat trials just down the road. The driver turned toward the research institute. We arrived after the staff had gone home for the day, the parking lot dust had settled, lights were out and all was quiet. Although I knew Noor's house, I'd been there often, I wanted just a personal moment with "my" wheat so we skirted the residences and headed straight out to the plots. The road ended at the field's edge. I asked the driver to wait there.

The evening settled softly, a warm blanket of silence reaching out across this research field. Behind a distant row of eucalyptus trees, the sun neared the horizon, reddened and dimmed by the Punjab's perpetual dust. Just outside the station fence, a mud-walled village lay, pulling its people home for the night. Dusky shadows slowly swallowed its streets and lanes. A lone farmer trudged behind his two bullocks as they followed by rote the path to their nighttime enclosure.

I walked out into my plots, our plots. Over a hundred different treatments grew there, each carefully replicated three times. As I walked, the call to prayer rose from a nearby mosque, praising Allah and inviting village men to their evening renewal of faith. Farther across the mud walls, a one-cylinder diesel engine started up, the whistle on its exhaust pipe telling village women that the mill was now open to grind their wheat for evening *roti*.

Within this bucolic scene, a peace settled over me. Only three years before, there had been no agronomic wheat research in Pakistan, and no on-farm trails. Yet here were acres of carefully designed, well run trials, their results beginning to show, results that farmers would duplicate in their own fields and then, hopefully adopt. Senior scientists had taken note, politicians had visited. After the germplasm in Mexipak, this was Step II in getting the nation's food deficit permanently solved.

It dawned on me that Pakistan's agricultural research programs would never again be the same. I couldn't help being swept up with a sense of pride, a feeling so intense that all other sensations ceased. For long seconds, it seemed like I was floating, some feet above these experimental plots, looking down at them. At that moment, it didn't matter if these experiments ever won a prize or garnered headlines. No one had to speak, or to validate anything. I just knew that what had happened here was fundamentally, permanently good. From across my plots, the mosque's metallic voice sang it all: *"Allahu Akbar."*

Part III: Into Africa

Into Africa

On leaving Pakistan, I faced a nagging question. If I had truly found a way out of poverty and income inequality by redirecting incomes and consumer power to the poor, shouldn't I be writing it up for the academic literature, contributing to the world's store of wisdom, the nature of global practice? "Saving the world" as we international development zealots were naively prone to say back then? Weren't there millions of folks out there, mired in poverty, who badly needed such a change in the course of their nation's programs?

But wait.

What if my findings only worked in Pakistan or, at most, South Asia? After all, this part of the world is culturally unique. Clearly, to have wider applications, to rise to the level of accepted development theory, my findings needed validation somewhere else under a different socio-economic environment. What exactly was this pattern that I thought should guide poverty reduction programs? Was it a one country artifact? Or was it more universal?

Severe inequality blights every sphere of cultural, religious, political and social life in India and Pakistan. If one looks closely, visitors such as I can't help but be struck by the extreme gaps all around us as we walk the streets, living out our daily lives. To an economist like me, trained in Keynesian theory, consumption spending drives the economy, and, here as elsewhere, the rich and poor spend their money in vastly different ways. That much is obvious and has informed decades of economic policy around the world. Also, the rural poor buy cheap goods because that's all they can afford. Again, we all know that.

But, in Pakistan's villages I found additional patterns, ties between people and households, which shape the lives of those living there. To me, the policy implication of these differing patterns was obvious – redistribute purchasing power to the lower income groups. Then let their spending drive the whole system and the rich could benefit as the economy blossomed. The job market would expand mostly hiring the poor and income gaps could begin to close. But, again, I needed to test these ideas with better data and in another cultural setting. Besides, I always wanted to work in Africa so here was my chance. The academic literature would just have to wait. I shoved any ideas of revising economic theory to the back burner and set out to field test the Pakistani answers somewhere else. Having never been to Africa, I naively thought that almost any African nation would be backward enough to provide a true acid test of my theory.

However, fate pitched me a curve ball. Lesotho, my first African country, had no really poor underclass. When I arrived there in 1977 they apparently had no millionaires either. With only one tribe (the Basotho), one language (Sesotho), a common history and culture, an area only the size of Maryland, and less than a million people, the country's economic structure was basically egalitarian. There would be no field test here. I concluded that my budding theory fit best in larger, more stratified societies where the poor and the rich could be identified in national statistics, where their ties to each other could be measured, and helpful policies designed.

However, with rural employment and poverty now on my résumé from the Pakistan years, the Government of Lesotho asked me to write the employment and labor chapters of their Third Five Year Plan. I did, producing chapters stressing small businesses and a vibrant small farm sector as engines of growth and job creation. Our Lesotho project produced a sweeping 20-year development plan filled with agricultural policy and program suggestions that could lead toward a more prosperous future. I wrote eighty percent of that document, USAID reproduced a thousand copies and when the project was over, those copies could be found in most offices in the Ministry of Agriculture or in Central Planning.

Our long term plans for rural development in Lesotho caught the attention of policy makers across the border in South Africa who were struggling to create jobs for their rural blacks as well. The laws, regulations, even the mind-set of apartheid stood clearly in their way. Toward the end of our Lesotho project, I was invited by the South African Prime Minister's office to address a small group of academics and policy advisors in Pretoria. They wanted to know whether Lesotho's lessons might also be useful to stimulate growth in their homelands, those hated "Bantustans" where blacks were forced to live if they didn't have a job in the so-called white areas and an official pass to get there.

I presented a paper that talked about greater skills and better job opportunities for rural black South Africans. I called for building more "basic needs infrastructure," something that was largely absent in areas where blacks were forced to live. This meant clinics, schools, water and sewage, electricity, paved roads, public transportation, all those services that whites took for granted. When I finished, a crusty, old-guard academic stood up in the back of the room, obviously intent on putting this "American expert" in his place.

"Dr. Eckert," he began. "You call for a Basic Needs approach which we all know costs a great deal. Do you realize that blacks comprise 80 percent of this country? We can't afford Basic Needs (this time he sneered the term) for all those people. Even if we spend the millions of Rand, all that we gain is that the blacks will remain quiet a little longer. I would suggest to you, Sir, that we could put half of those same funds into the Police and Defense Forces and we would keep the blacks just as quiet." An uneasy stirring rippled through the room.

Dr. Piet du Toit, the national Director of Policy Analysis and, by then, a colleague and friend, chaired that session. He leapt to the podium interjecting, "Jerry, you do not have to respond to that." He knew I was being baited.

"Piet, I would like nothing better than to answer that," I replied, leaning into the microphone to cause a slight rise in volume. My antagonist had thrown down a gauntlet and raised the stakes. Of course I would respond. Maybe now I could get my basic point across to this group which included some of the central players in South Africa's policy dialogue. The murmur in the room quickly subsided.

"Gentlemen." I continued. "There is a poverty crisis in this country. There is another, related crisis — income inequality. Because of apartheid, the gaps between rich and poor in South Africa are the worst ever measured for any nation, anywhere."

Most of them did not know that fact so I let it sink in for a moment. Then I quoted from their own 10 Year Development Programme which admitted that they had no redistributive policies because they did not understand the underlying causes of income inequality. They had never studied the unique and suppressing dynamics, the few opportunities, the staggering impediments faced by black household heads in their own country.

"You can't expect the bottom of the income spectrum to remain quiet and accept their lot forever. Their current situation is, in many cases, inhumane. So, my response to you, Sir, is that if you don't do something about income inequality pretty soon, it won't matter how much money you put into the Defense Force. The lid is going to blow off this place, violently and irretrievably." Again I paused. The audience was silent, mulling my blunt prediction.

As an afterthought, I added, "What you really need to do is invest some money into generating knowledge. Find out how your black population behaves economically, how they relate to the mainstream white economy, to private business and to government. What policy levers do you have to improve their salaries and wages? Then, maybe you can make some informed choices that will lead to a better quality of life for your blacks in the longer term."

* * *

Looking back, that may have been a turning point for South Africa. A small one, perhaps. Unheralded? Certainly. But a turning point nonetheless. Among those sitting there were senior staff in the Office of the Economic Advisor to Prime

Minister Botha. Seven months later, I was sitting in my university office back in Colorado preparing a lecture when the phone rang. It was my friend, Dawie Mullins, South Africa's Director of Planning, calling from Pretoria.

"We did it, Jerry." I heard excitement in his voice. "We found the money for the research you wanted. We are ready to start the project. Will you lead it?"

I was elated. But worried as well. At that time, U.S. and British universities enforced an academic boycott of South Africa, refusing all exchanges, of students, faculty, research collaboration – everything, to protest South Africa's segregated higher education. This posturing seemed to me rather ironic. South Africa's segregated universities were modeled on the U.S. Second Morrill Act of 1890 which, rather than integrate our white universities, established a parallel system now known as the 1890 schools or Historically Black Universities. Yes, America has since rejected "separate but equal" as bad theory and a gross injustice. But not South Africa, at least not in 1981. Given the boycott, would I be allowed to go? Could I work directly for the Prime Minister of this "apartheid regime" without somehow being punished back on my own campus? Neither my Department Head nor Dean wanted to touch that question so I wandered over to the office of the university president, Phil Austin, and explained my dilemma.

"Jerry, if you can have a greater impact working for change within that system than you would attacking it from outside, then go. Do it! I'll cover your ass here at home," he said.

I shook his hand, promised that he would not regret his decision and left. Between Austin's office and mine stands a grove of trees the students call Sherwood Forest. The pines there are tall and close with cooling shade beneath. I entered this silent place and sat down on a bench. Ahead lay a chance to influence a whole nation, to help one of my favorite countries move beyond their racism, and elevate their black people to a better life. My breathing slowed as the enormity of my possible future challenges settled around me.

* * *

Ten days later I was in Pretoria negotiating what became a six year research effort. South Africa contracted with Colorado State University for me to work part-time in their Prime Minister's offices. Under Dawie's leadership, we pulled together a team of South African economists, an American graduate student and me. Most of the data we needed were available, scattered around, often in inconsistent formats or hidden away in obscure places. Some of it, however, had never been imagined, much less collected. For the next three years we assembled, created, examined, and played with numbers to discover new insights on how the races connected to each other and to the overall economy. In the end, a view emerged of a tightly interlocked web of relationships across the population, a view that helped change attitudes across South Africa.

South Africa turned out to be the next best country after than India with the conditions I needed to validate my Pakistani findings; extreme income inequality and a very dense set of raw data on personal incomes and spending habits. And it was far enough removed culturally from the Indo-Pakistan subcontinent to provide my acid test.

The policy of apartheid segregated everything. In 1980 approximately 85 percent of the population was "Non-White," a hated classification, defining people by what they were not. This label included blacks, people of mixed race, those of Indian or Malay descent, and Khoi-san Bushmen. Laws and rules beyond counting severely restricted access to jobs, education, places to live, who you could marry for anyone who was not fully Caucasian or more narrowly European. These policies demoralized and impoverished millions. Apartheid law also rusticated, almost imprisoned, many blacks into underdeveloped, overcrowded "homelands."

To see for myself, I went to homelands like Qwaqwa, Bophutatswana and KwaZulu. There I found rural economies that worked much like my Punjabi villages had. Busy women sold live chickens or garden produce out of their back doors. Old widows brewed sorghum beer in great pottery vats for the men home on leave from their jobs outside their homeland. Other women traveled to the city on the bus and brought back minuscule lots of household sundries which they retailed to their neighbors. Small children tended the family livestock. Working age men were mostly absent, having migrated to jobs in the cities or the mines where they had permits to work. Their remittances provided spending money for their families in the homelands. The women left behind were ingenious, finding myriad niches in which to make a little something extra. For some it was critical, like the widows with their sorghum beer. These monies then circulated within the local village from one low income household to another.

I made a second discovery among South Africa's poor. Urban townships, such as Soweto near Johannesburg or

Kayelitsha outside Cape Town, in which urban blacks were forced by law to live, were a lot like a rural village but in compressed form. Urban black townships usually had the advantage of electricity and public transportation which opened a wider array of home business options. While formal artisan castes did not exist, informally it was much the same as Pakistan, with barbers, baby sitters, cooks, bar owners, washer women, blacksmiths, carpenters, seamstresses, and the rest.

Our research focused on income inequality and poverty in order to come up with a vision, policy prescriptions really, that might change things for the better. We chose a Social Accounting Matrix (SAM) pioneered by the World Bank as our analytical tool because it highlights spending behaviors of any selected group of households. We could see how money spent by each category created jobs and incomes for other households, how it affected tax receipts, investment savings, imports, and the broader economy as a whole. It is a powerful tool. Our SAM looked at seven income classes within each of four races, more household detail than any SAM ever built, anywhere. If you wanted to know whose income or jobs would rise if, say, an upper income white South African bought a pair of shoes, this model could answer that. If someone in New York consumed a bottle of Pinotage, produced for export in a vineyard in Stellenbosch, the model told how much of that bottle's price paid Black labor in Cape Province, how much paid for Coloured labor, how much went to the White vineyard owner, even how much was paid to the farmer in Portugal who grew the cork that stoppered the bottle. And not only would the model show wages by race, it showed how poor or affluent the wage recipients were. And then we could track the effects of the spending of each group receiving new incomes from that bottle of Pinotage in New York. If you wanted to see the effects of an extra $10 in the pocket of a poor Black man or a middle income Coloured, the model answered that clearly as well.

It was also dicey work, done with minimal publicity. In order for our results to have much effect, I felt that the model and the analyses that flowed from it needed to be widely available for use by anyone. But the bureaucrats balked. Anti-apartheid activists abroad clamored for punitive sanctions against South Africa. Our SAM could be used in reverse, showing which international actions, trade sanctions for example, would reduce white incomes most severely. Indeed, not long afterward, an over-zealous academic at Denver University tried just that but nobody paid him any attention. In Pretoria, no one in government wanted to be that one person who made the report public. Finally, Prime Minister P.W. Botha, the man who had once declared to his white electorate, "We must adapt or die," ordered our report released and made freely available to every economist and policy analyst in the country. His economic advisor convened a meeting of economists whose views carried weight in Pretoria. They flew me in from Colorado as keynote speaker. For most of a full day Davie and I presented the model's results which strongly supported a national emphasis on income redistribution.

The doubters said, "If you give money to the poor, they will spend it all and save nothing. And they pay no taxes. Without savings and taxes there will be no investment funds for future growth." However, the SAM showed that spending by the poor provided enough stimuli to business that business and corporate savings and taxes would offset the lower personal savings.

South Africa's economy was closely tied to gold exports, narrowly based and languishing with growth rates slowly shrinking toward zero. The SAM suggested that redistributing incomes to the poor would keep their spending circulating within the country and that additional domestic consumer spending could become the driver of economic growth, effectively replacing gold.

Unemployment among blacks exceeded 20 percent in those days; some estimates put it as high as 45 percent. The more labor intensive nature of what the poor would buy offered a partial solution to that as well.

After that meeting I went back to Dawie's house, drank a cold beer, and then went for a walk alone. At that moment, everything had come together. All the pieces fit and the result was unprecedented. South Africa would never again be the same. They could never again ignore the economic plight of the poorer classes or the income inequality that was so pervasive. It was one of those out-of-body moments. I know I walked around the block, but my mind floated in another place. Something good had happened and I was privileged to have been a part of it.

Mahlapane's Story

A slanting blade of yellow light sliced through the cracks of a hand-made door, slid across my face and jarred me awake. Around me, rough-hewn stone formed the walls of the rondavel, the traditional round hut of southern African villages. Overhead a roof of thatching grass kept morning chills at bay, sealing in the smells of last night's smoky cooking fire. I had spent the night in Ha Potsane, a village of perhaps 300 households, perched on the grassy slopes of Lesotho's lowlands. It had been a fitful night in an unfamiliar bed. Insects from the thatch above had left a sprinkling of welts across my exposed skin. I rose and stood in the doorway, stretching out the cramps. The air brought whiffs of dew and dung smoke. At each rondavel, cotton white plumes from breakfast fires escaped through vents and crevices, then snaked downward through the village, hugging the ground, past a spring where a pair of horses drank, and out across the valley below. Small stirrings here and there – children's voices, a pot being scraped – told of a new day.

I had recently arrived in Lesotho, a nation on the southern African map no larger than Maryland. I was leading a team of academics who would spend the next three years strengthening the capabilities of young professionals in the Ministry of Agriculture. This was my first African assignment. Everything about this land was new to me. I had much to learn.

I brought with me a driving commitment to helping the poor. For eight years I had worked in Pakistan where income inequality was extreme – where twenty million Pakistanis lived on ten U.S. cents a day while twenty-two families of industrialists averaged incomes of $4,000 an hour for each family member. I watched these inequities crush the vitality from villagers' lives and destabilize their government. I lived with them in their villages, shared their meals of flat bread, tea and a boiled egg because that's all there was, and heard their anguish over whether their children might ever imagine something better. Then I wrote policy prescriptions that offered a possible way out for Pakistan. Now I wondered if these policies might also be needed in Lesotho. To answer this, I needed to find and to understand Lesotho's poverty if I could.

I had to get out of the capital city, visit a village and meet people who rode Basotho ponies to work instead of polished black limousines. In an accident of perfect timing, I met an American, Judy Gay, who was researching women's roles in village life for her doctorate in economic anthropology. She kept a rondavel in Ha Potsane as her field research base. In Ha Potsane, as elsewhere across Lesotho, women head seventy percent of families. As an added bonus for Judy, the regional chief, a woman of influence and grace and a member of the royal family, lived here and ruled from her substantial compound. When Judy invited me to spend a few days in her village, I leapt at the chance. I didn't realize it yet but what I knew of Africa was about to change.

We drove out to her village in time for an evening meal of corn grits, beef sausage and tomato gravy. Then it was early to bed – our work would begin at daybreak.

94

The next morning, Judy and I took off across the village to meet with some of the women whose lives and thoughts she was recording. We threaded our way through a bleating flock of iridescent white mohair goats, kicked a rolling soccer ball back toward some laughing urchins, and ducked under a clothesline hung with laundry. I tagged along, all eyes and ears, hoping my presence wouldn't bias her conversations. Judy was uncovering nuances of power linked to social and kinship relations. She seemed to be on anthropology's cutting edge, and I pestered her with questions. But the lesson from that visit that still humbles me today came from an unexpected source.

Mahlapane was a wisp of a girl with a shy smile, penetrating eyes and a recent high school diploma. At 19, she was exactly half my age. She worked as Judy's research assistant, making introductions, translating from Sesotho, and explaining deeper meanings of what was said. Her real strength as a research partner came from her insider status in this village. She knew these people intimately, knew their individual stories, their collective history. During my visit, she hung around Judy's rondavel after work, mostly making small talk. Maybe she was just curious to see who this new white guy was, the stranger who had come to her village from abroad, and to figure out just why he was here.

We spent that first day in interviews. I sat hunched on the edge of conversations on rondavel stoops, trying to be invisible, even though I was being ogled by big-eyed, half-naked children. By quitting time, I wasn't sure if I was any closer to finding real poverty in Lesotho although I thought I had seen some hints. Some women wore dresses purchased new in South Africa while others made do with ill-fitting hand-me-downs. Some horses were well fed, others scrawny. Some children were nicely dressed and clean, others wore mostly rags and street dust. A few houses had corrugated metal roofs but most were only thatched with grass. I hoped that Mahlapane might explain these things to me.

That evening, we three sat on the stoop of Judy's rondavel in the still, balmy air. Shadows gradually stretched dark fingers across the open grasslands in front of us. Judy and I were relaxed, Mahlapane a little less so. She wore a crisply pressed blue dress, not unlike a school uniform. Although she didn't say much, she followed our banter intently. I brought the conversation around to poverty and then asked her directly,

"Mahlapane, what makes people poor in this village?" My question drew a quizzical silence. I tried another tack.

"Look, aren't there people in Ha Potsane that you would consider poor?"

"What do you mean by 'poor'?"

Judy tried to help, searching for just the right words in the Sesotho language. Mahlapane didn't think there were poor people in her village. I still didn't think she understood the question. There had to be a few of them. The conversation staggered a bit while the foreign expert and the village girl tried to reach common ground.

Then I spied what I thought would be my Rosetta Stone. Down the lane from our left shuffled a rather gaunt older man leading three horses out toward evening pasture. He wore a tattered coat, frayed at the cuffs, one sleeve partly detached. His patched trousers had seen many days since their last washing. His unwashed hair looked ratty as it fell around his weathered unshaven face. When he greeted us, we saw his missing teeth.

"There!" I whispered. "Isn't that man poor?"

"Oh, No. That's Ntate Thabong."

She emphasized his last name slightly. Thabong was not her relative, so her use of "Ntate," Sesotho for "father," showed the cultural deference reserved for respected older men. Still, just his name did not help with the poverty question. Which must have shown in my eyes, because, after a pause she added,

"He is the chief's groom. Those are the chief's horses."

We watched the slow parade out to pasture while I digested her information. The horses seemed more eager than did Ntate Thabong. The procession paused at the little spring just beyond our hut. The horses snuffled up some water, smacked the drops from their lips, and nodded their muzzles up and down.

Mahlapane broke the silence.

"Ntate Thabong's father was groom to the previous chief. And his father's father was groom to Chief Goliath."

This last bit was important. Everyone remembered Chief Goliath, a powerful leader in the old days when chiefs had power to wield. Even I had read his name, though he had been dead for years. In fact, this village had once been named Ha Goliath, the place of Goliath. In my mind, Ntate Thabong was no longer a simple tender of horses. Instead he held a hereditary position of trust and honor, intimately tied to regional chiefs and through the royal lineage, however remotely, to His Majesty, King Moshoeshoe II.

"But," I persisted, "he looks like he doesn't even have enough money for food."

97

"He eats at the Chief's kitchen," she said without elaboration.

"So which one is his rondavel?"

"He sleeps in a room at the Chief's compound."

I made one final attempt.

"But with all that, just look at him. Isn't he still poor?"

Mahlapane looked at me, I would like to think wistfully, but it may have been with sadness. This village girl with her high school diploma then turned squarely to the international expert with his doctorate and his theories and simply said:

"A man is only poor if he knows he is poor."

It took a while, but once her statement sank in, I truly saw Ntate Thabong for the first time.

Though he never spoke to me directly, Ntate Thabong left me with a question that has guided my values for years. Just what is it that underpins a person's sense of self worth, of personal dignity, of knowing that he or she matters? Maybe these two, the old man and the girl together, were my Rosetta Stone after all; the unreadable, shuffling hieroglyph and the translator who changed him into words I understood.

This unshaven man with missing teeth likely had no money in his pocket. Yet he also had no worries over food or shelter. He was clothed, if not well. He ate, slept, worked and moved freely about in the center of local power and authority. He had an important patron whom he served faithfully. In the traditional horse culture of Lesotho, one's horse, tack and regalia form essential parts of rank and reputation. If he did his job with skill, his Chief was well mounted. His job made him a local cultural icon. He and his family had been linked to the lineage of chiefs for generations from which he drew respect and pride. Because of these things, everyone in the village knew his name and addressed him as Ntate. What need had he for money or property? His name, his job and the respect of his village were property enough.

It has been many years since I lived in that part of Africa. Yet still today, a short, moving image of this shuffling man with the chief's three horses replays itself often in my head. I see the blend of dust and brown clothes, his weathered skin and his plodding pace. I hear the horses slup up water, see the drops fall from their lips. I can hear their first bites as they start their evening meal on the grassy slope that fronts Ha Potsane. And in the background, the sound track for my mental video is Mahlapane's voice,

"A man is only poor if he knows he is poor."

Saddle Leather and Protocol

Breakfast in Judy's rondavel the next morning was *phutu pap*, a crumbly mound of steamed white corn grits with a delightful smoky flavor. We were scraping breakfast dishes when a shout froze us for a second. After a pause, the shouting continued, picked up a rhythm, added some high notes and low. Almost a song, it was stern but not panicked, a lyrical command voice. Judy listened a moment longer.

"That's the village crier," she interpreted. "We have about half an hour to get ready."

All my life I had heard of town criers, an essential part of village communities before people could read, before radio and newspapers. To me, the idea of a town crier suggested earlier times in medieval Europe or colonial America. Yet here was one in the flesh, wrapped against the morning chill in his blanket, doing his crying through the lanes and rondavels, the round stone houses, of Ha Potsane. The village was being called to assemble. I was electrified, my senses riveted by this living relic of a day I had thought long gone.

* * *

November is late spring in the southern hemisphere. Lesotho's famous peach trees had bloomed a month earlier, their myriad small fruits now swelling. Early vegetables such as peas and onions poked new leaves into sunlight in a first burst of serious growth. Normally on such a spring day farmers would plow the hillsides and plant hybrid maize seeds brought in from South Africa to ensure their household staple food. In these heavy soils, it often takes two teams of scrawny cows, whipped from behind and hauled by a halter from the front, to drag a single-bottomed plow across a sloping field. Today, however, both cows and plowmen would rest. Today was set aside for politics and ceremony. A day to let an ancient culture flourish and to nourish roles and kinships imbedded in tradition. The chief of the region, a woman named Malitha, would journey by horseback from her home and office complex in Ha Potsane well up on the mountainside to install Malesa, another woman, as the new chief in that remote village. Judy and I had been invited to ride along. Since both chiefs were female, this could be a significant day for Judy's research on women's roles in village culture.

A herdsman brought two horses, already saddled, to our rondavel. We then led them to an open space that served double duty as village square and royal courtyard in front of Malitha's home. Over the next half hour, 50 to 60 people gathered there in small knots, some smoking, some examining each other's ponies, some talking politics. Like the day before, the aroma of morning cow dung cooking fires escaped from nearby homes and crept across this plaza. We waited. Even in Ha Potsane the woman in charge could take her time getting ready.

Lesotho is a nation of horsemen. There are few roads in the mountains and foothills. Horseback travel is often the only alternative to walking. Over the centuries, the Basotho pony has earned special status in Sesotho culture. A man's personal identity requires that he be well mounted and ride with skill. These ponies are sure-footed and hardy, combining legendary endurance with gentleness. They are ridden, often rapidly, straight up and down precipitous inclines. They are rarely shod. They have a unique gait known locally as a "triple" or "triplicate," a unique three-beat lateral gait, slightly faster than a trot. When a pony breaks into a triple, it's a moment of true equestrian grace. The rider sweeps across the landscape, body held erect, head tracing a smooth horizontal line, suspended above his mount's amazing pattern of tricky footwork.

Most of those now assembled led or sat their ponies. Few of the mounts in this motley herd showed the classic muscular, partly Arabian conformation of a true Basotho pony. However, each rider took obvious pride in his mount. Saddles had been cleaned, saddle blankets shaken out or washed. The people, as well, were groomed and dressed for something special. Most wore the expected blue Basotho blanket. At the end of the 19th century, as game was hunted to extinction, wild hides for garments became rare. Enterprising South African traders brought in blankets, usually blue, to wear as cloaks. One hundred years later, blankets are now considered traditional garb.

To vent his excitement, or maybe just to pass the time showing off, one man gave a shout, booted his pony into a quick triple across a hundred yards or so, then abruptly pulled his horse back onto its heels, kicking up dust all around. His buddies shouted their approval.

After half an hour or more, an older man mounted up and called on the rest of us to do the same. Once in our saddles, we all flowed toward what seemed to be predetermined places in the village plaza. Judy and I were shown to the rear of this procession. A woman appeared on the stoop of the chief's home and a hush descended. All eyes turned to her. She was the chief's attendant, her lady-in-waiting.

Then slowly, deliberately, Malitha, chief of the region, emerged. Dressed in a billowing floor-length orange dress with a bright blue Basotho blanket around her shoulders, she flowed, seemingly without effort, across the stoop. She was, after all, a member of the Ba Koena, People of the Crocodile, Lesotho's royal family, and she moved with regal grace. Two women helped her descend the stairs to the plaza. She crossed to her pony, which Ntate Thabong, her personal groom, held proudly in the middle of the crowd. A stool appeared next to the animal. Assisted by attendants, she mounted. Sitting straight in the saddle, she bent slightly to give some final instructions to her groom. Her lady-in-waiting mounted and took a place beside and just behind Malitha. A few others adjusted their positions. We were ready.

From the front, a hundred yards ahead of Judy and me, a high-pitched quavering voice rang out. Heading the group, an older man, probably Ha Potsane's town crier, launched into a praise poem, blessing and dignifying this event. As we rode across the next half-mile, he would weave an oral tapestry of local history unbroken from earliest tribal memories. His shouted poem touched on locally important events; the rinderpest plague of 1897, the killing drought of the 1930s, the battles, the coronations that gave this village its legacy. He counted down the complete lineage of national Kings and honored previous chiefs ending with Chief Malitha, recognized as the reigning leader, essentially the princess of Ha Potsane.

A shout rang out and we were underway. Almost as one, our throng of horses surged forward. Within a few paces, most were in a canter. A few broke into their famous triple. The sound of hooves became a drum roll, thundering beneath the praise poet's song. Then, along the pathway leading from the village, a wild joyous ululation swept out across the riders. Throats keened in the shrill wavering cry so characteristic of southern Africa. Village women lined the path, arms raised, hands waving in celebration, their cry an aural blanket cast over their horsemen and their princess. For long moments, the world of Ha Potsane dissolved into a dusty blur of motion, colors and sound, mostly sound. From higher up, sandstone bluffs caught three voices from our group, a rolling thunder base, a tenor prayer and a great soprano chorus of joy, mixed them up and threw them back as echoes upon this royal procession.

For half a mile the group kept up the pace. Then as we crossed a broad plain, the riders spread out. Some rode in the lead, others on the sides, Judy, some younger men and I brought up the rear in a knot. Seen from above, our procession would have resembled a spear point, tipped by the town crier, its cutting edges formed by younger men riding flank, its base narrowed and flattened across the back. In the middle of this cantering wedge rode Malitha, her lady in waiting and an older male advisor or two. This formation broke down only when the trail finally narrowed. Even then, Malitha rode in the middle of a line of her subjects, seemingly protected, both fore and aft.

We rode for a couple of hours, well settled into ancient rhythms. The sun rose pushing aside the morning chill. New verdure stippled the countryside in expectant shades of green. Leaving the cultivated plains behind, we climbed into foothills dotted with herd boys and their flocks of crystalline white mohair goats. Conversations in Sesotho, unintelligible to me, became background harmonies to the drumbeat of unshod hooves and the weathered voice of creaking leather. As we passed through smaller villages, women lined our path again, arms raised, their ululations showering Malitha and the procession with tribute. After five miles the trail pitched steeply up a slope, carried us over a rise and dumped us abruptly into the middle of the village of Ralefatla. Again a stool appeared and Chief Malitha dismounted with grace. Malesa, soon to be installed as village chief, greeted her deferentially. The two of them disappeared into a nearby rondavel, leaving the rest of us to disperse throughout the village in search of friends or things to do.

* * *

Joala, a sorghum beer, forms a staple of the southern Sotho diet. *Joala* is an acquired taste. With a consistency of watery porridge, its gray-brown color of regurgitated oatmeal, and a musty flavor of spoiled grain suffused with hints of acid and alcohol, *joala* is an acquired taste. Nutritionists claim it's also good food, laced with proteins, carbohydrates, B vitamins and iron. Traditional wisdom attributes medicinal values as well, including, some say, aphrodisiac powers. Within the village economy, *joala* redistributes income and fights poverty. Old widows with no income do most of the brewing and men, on leave from their South African jobs with cash in their pockets, are their main customers. More than this, *joala* is a southern Sotho cultural icon, one of the glues in human relations and an expected part of village cultural celebrations. The widows of Ralefatla had been busy. For three days earthen vats had fermented their secret recipes. Smiling eyes betrayed their pride as Judy and I were handed our half-quart mugs of their final product.

Judy sought out some local women to ask about their lives with their men out of the country. Mug in hand, yet linguistically excluded, I wandered alone among the rondavels, watching from the sidelines this living tableau that basically ignored me. I felt like a secret observer, rather like wealthy Italians in da Vinci's time, sequestered in their *camera obscuras*, watching slow village street scenes upside-down and backwards. I saw herd boys take ponies out to graze. Old men, shoulders wrapped in blankets, played a form of checkers using pebbles on a grid etched crudely onto a flat protruding rock. People sat in clusters here and there, talking and laughing, about what, I did not know. A beef animal had been slaughtered and a Sotho specialty, stewed organ meats with wild spinach, cooked slowly in a great metal pot over a dung chip fire.

How little had things changed here on this isolated hillside in the century or more since the first paramount chief, Moshoeshoe I, coalesced a bunch of scattered family groups and villages into a community of people and called it a nation? Local stone and thatching grass turned into homes, cow dung provided heating and cooking energy. In Ralefatla, only the people's clothes and a few tools and house wares came from outside the village. We were miles from electricity, roads, vehicles, the media, fossil fuels – miles from the trappings of modern life. Today's installation would reprise a ceremony not unlike what Moshoeshoe I might have used to unite his nation. Malitha would invest Malesa with her rights and responsibilities as chief of Ralefatla. Malesa would swear fealty directly to Malitha, the regional chief, and through her to the paramount chief, His Majesty Moshoeshoe II.

Ultimately a chief must earn respect and legitimacy with her ability to listen to the people, to hear their grievances or aspirations and to negotiate solutions that satisfy everyone. Such a chieftainship forms a representative government, almost a pure democracy. And it used to work that way. Now, unfortunately, only vestiges of the chiefs' original power and roles remain. However, revisiting them in ceremony, such as we would do today, keeps those vestiges alive and with them renews the culture and heritage of the Basotho people.

Around noon, the socializing stopped; the two villages came together under a canvas awning. Malitha and the elders spoke briefly, signed documents, and shook hands. A spontaneous burst of ululation and it was done. Ralefatla had a new chief. The meal began. Everyone filled their plates with meat, entrails and potatoes. Politics were over for the day and friends and neighbors turned to the pleasant conviviality of a village feast on the side of a remote mountain, anchored in Lesotho's cultural past.

* * *

A couple of hours later, after a final mug of *joala*, it was time to leave. Herd boys rounded up our mounts, the two chiefs embraced, Malitha was assisted into her saddle, and our procession lined out down the trail toward Ha Potsane. Again, when the trail widened, the spear point formed around Malitha. Again, Judy and I brought up the rear.

About a mile short of our destination, Judy called me out of formation and we rode off toward a nearby stream. She wanted to show me where she and some village women had planted an irrigated garden that was just beginning to produce spring vegetables. As we returned to the trail, we heard shouts in the distance. Well ahead, the whole procession had halted. They were ordering us to get back into formation where we belonged. Everyone, the regional chief and all, waited. Our indiscretion embarrassed me. We, the invited outsiders, had violated an unwritten taboo and brought the whole afternoon to an inglorious halt. Judy and I broke into a furious gallop. Desperately, I grabbed my saddle's pommel. It really would be bad form for the "foreign expert" to become unhorsed in front of the whole entourage. We caught up and were motioned into our positions at the rear. Was it my imagination, or were they less polite about it this time? As we took up our final cantor into Ha Potsane, to my amazement, the spear point had reformed. Into the village with rolling thunder and a cloud of dust we swept, delivering Malitha right up to the courtyard of her home.

Our excursion into Lesotho's distant past was over. My time machine, a borrowed Basotho pony, plodded to a halt right where we started, back in the present again. Every bit of that day, from the first shout of the village crier, to his praise poem as we rode out, the celebratory ululations, the sounds of a mounted tribe thundering up the valley, a regal ceremony legitimized by feasting and sorghum beer, to the post-gallop sweat now coating my pony's flanks could have been last year or last century. Clearly rural Lesotho today remains deeply rooted in its tribal past, a continuity that undoubtedly brings moral strength and collective pride.

* * *

For a long time afterward I wondered about that flying wedge of mounted horsemen and why the village had insisted that proper decorum required everyone to be in their rightful place. Some years later, reading of another social group in motion, it dawned on me that perhaps I had been caught up in something much older than just Lesotho's history.

Irven DeVore spent his lifetime studying primate biology, sociology and the evolution of intelligence. Grounded in decades of global fieldwork, DeVore's influence was once considered seminal. One of his much-cited works details social behavior among baboons. In it, I found my spear point, a geometric positioning of members of a baboon troop as they move though the African savannah. DeVore claimed this pattern was "invariable in all groups observed. Mothers carrying their infants tend to be found in the middle of a group when it is on the move; the less dominant males are to the front, at the sides and to the rear; and the most dominant males are (also) in the middle. This places the most vulnerable (mothers with infants and young children) at the center, within and around the most dominant and protective adult males." A young adult male "sentinel" often precedes the group by 200 to 400 yards. At his alarm bark, one or more of the large adult males will move to the front to examine the disturbance, a behavior that was "observed consistently in all groups both in the Cape (South Africa) and in Kenya." In this way, the group's most important assets, its breeding females and their progeny, are protected. The sentinel, the voice of the group, forms the point of the spear.

Had I not seen this formation before? In Lesotho, yes. But also in descriptions of 19th century wagon trains on the

Oregon or Santa Fe trails. Scouts on point, outriders on the flanks, a rear guard of young men riding drag at the back, and in the wagons at the center, the valuables – women, children and grandma's spinning wheel brought all the way from Kentucky.

Devore stresses that defense of those assets most vital to the group's survival lie behind the spear point formation. For baboons moving through leopard habitat or wagon trains in Indian country, this need is obvious. Yet Malitha and the men and women of Ha Potsane were not threatened. Malitha was surrounded, almost cocooned, out of respect for her position and whatever personal esteem she may have earned. Survival's needs have evolved. Protection had become deference and deference became respect. It was no accident that Judy and I, hangers-on at the periphery of this society, were back there in the dust riding drag. We were placed there. It was proper. It was protocol. So much so that a broken formation returning out of the traditional past to Ha Potsane could not be tolerated.

Hail Doctors

Not long after our arrival in Lesotho, the CSU team took our first field trip. Manapo, our boss and head of the Planning Division invited us to a welcoming feast in her family's village home some 30 miles out of town. She wanted us to meet her family and experience a taste of traditional village life in her corner of Africa. A narrow dirt track led from Lesotho's only paved highway into her village, winding through fields of maize dotted with an under story of white-skinned pumpkins. Mixed breed cattle grazed the grassy patches, looked after by herd boys. Our chunky Chevy Blazers, forced on us by the U.S. government's "Buy American" policy, looked very much out of place. Those cubes of robin's-egg blue raised dust traces in their wake across an ochre and brown landscape.

Half a mile before Manapo's village, we passed a solitary rondavel. I wondered why that one home stood out here on a ridge all by itself. Woven wire fencing surrounded a small bare earth yard and a garden plot. Two or three sheep huddled in a corner, jostling nervously as we approached. Alongside the garden, a woman busied herself at her clothesline hanging white sheets and towels to dry. It was late morning, maybe 11:00, under a brilliant sky. Overhead, small puffs of white cloud drifted aimlessly, like popcorn in the bottom of an upturned blue bowl.

"Oh boy. She's asking for trouble," I said. All eyes turned toward this lady's house.

"Why?" one of my passengers asked.

"Didn't you read your orientation material?" I asked. "Traditional Sotho belief holds that hanging out white laundry in the middle of the day attracts hail." Waving my hand at fields of maize, I added, "A good hail storm could make a mess out of all that." Around us, maize had reached the soft kernel phase, young enough to be picked and roasted like sweet corn over charcoal, but not yet ready to be harvested for grain. I was joking, or so I thought, by suggesting that this woman's laundry might actually trigger a hailstorm. Some of these more fanciful village beliefs amazed me.

As we pulled up to the edge of the village, a throng of animated young boys surged around our cars, each elbowing their way to the front of the pack, under instructions from the adults to intercept us and lead us to the festivities. But not before they cried out the common children's chant, "You give me sweets, mister? You give me five cents?" To Manapo's chagrin and embarrassment, Lesotho's children play this happy game with visitors everywhere. This time, however, they lost out since we had brought neither small change nor hard candy.

One of the older boys, all of seven years old perhaps, stood erect, very serious and said, "You come with me." Feeling very important, he led his six overseas charges to a large thatch-roofed rondavel, maybe 60 feet in diameter, which served as the village community center.

Manapo, with all her personal sparkle, met us at the door. She was resplendent in a long flowing orange and red print dress with matching headdress. This was not the official Manapo who had met us at the airport on arrival. This Manapo beamed, laughed and kept several conversations going at once. This was Manapo at home. Chairs ringed the inner edge of the rondavel, some of them empty, waiting for us to sit and meet her extended family. Manapo kept busy with introductions, translations, and explanations of who was who. The only awkward moments came when a language barrier arose. Necessarily, most men in Lesotho learn basic Afrikaans as their second language because they must find work in South Africa. Few men master more than rudimentary English although most of the women did.

Manapo also supervised sisters, cousins and friends at the cookstove. On a table in the center of the room, grew aromatic heaps of traditional foods. Hearty steam bread made from sorghum, *Phutu pap* - maize grits cooked dry and smoky, *boerewors* - a strongly seasoned beef sausage, grilled chops of well-fatted sheep, sweet red-fleshed pumpkin. In one corner stood a clay vat of thick sorghum beer, the first I'd ever tasted. As guests of honor, we could not refuse the special delicacy in the center of the table, a delicious traditional stew of sheep organs, kidneys, liver, tongue and testicles, turned greenish-black with wild spinach. With regal serenity, for, after all, she also was royal family, Manapo's mother sat with two friends off to one side, watching her daughter's special day unfold.

After a filling lunch, some of the men and I went for a walk through the maize fields to look at their crops. They showed me a promising new hybrid but complained about the price of seed they had to pay across the border in South Africa. We talked of fertilizers and maize borers and rain. We smoked our cigarettes to stave off the torpor brought on by full bellies.

A flock of sheep grazed on a distant hillock casually watched by an ever-present herd boy. Among the snow white dots, a black lump stood out. I had noticed that flocks often contained a black sheep or black and tan in the mix. I knew that British colonialists had made off-colored sheep an issue, culling every one they found so that Lesotho could export pure white Merino fleece. Now, eleven years after Independence, the genetic admixture had again swept the country and Lesotho's lower quality wool crop brought poor prices, sometimes selling only as junk fiber to the felt market.

"Why do you keep a black sheep in every flock? Doesn't that lower the class of wool you can sell?" I was curious. Why did this practice continue since the costs were well known?

"Mostly they're wethers, castrated rams." I was told. "We keep them in the flock to draw the lightning away from the white ones. It's a good system. When lightning kills a black one, we eat well. If it kills a white sheep, we lose money."

"And that works?"

"Most definitely." I was assured. *Note to self: Since most traditional beliefs have some basis in fact, however obscure, try to find out the physics behind this one.*

Seven or eight miles away reared an escarpment, which everyone in Lesotho calls the "Foothills." From north to south along the country's entire length, 2,000 feet of sandstone cliffs rise abruptly from the arable lowlands to grassy pasture lands above. In summer, warm air sweeps up this rock face, then races even higher, towering into thunder heads that can reach to 30,000 feet and more. When conditions are right, which happens often, air begins a whipsaw ride, carrying tiny droplets up to freeze, down to wet again in the moist base of the cloud, then up to freeze another layer. These hail seeds ride their roller coaster until they are too big to rise any more. Then all hell breaks loose.

Today would be one such day. First the breeze chilled as we lost the sun. Cotton-candy clouds above the mountains turned gray. Somebody said it would be all right because their hail doctor, reputedly the region's most powerful, had been well paid.

But that day, literally as we watched, those clouds turned black and begin to boil. That storm started off the mountain heading straight toward us. Lightning sizzled along the cliffs while we double-timed it back to the rondavel. Ominous words that I couldn't understand were shouted in Sesotho.

When the storm hit, hailstones and rain pellets flew sideways. Two or three apricot trees leaned with the wind, straining as if to tear their roots out. Thunder explosions followed lightning strikes almost instantly, shaking the plates of leftovers. Debris flew past the window, accompanied by a loose bucket bouncing along. Rivulets formed through the village, became freshets, and then a spate of floating hailstones and slop. A goat, forgotten at its tether in the courtyard, bleated in panic.

We stood at the rondavel door watching. Some of the women held each other. Kids clustered at their knees, eyes wide and staring. Men stood in grim silence. Cold damp air permeated everything and those who had one handy, wrapped themselves in a traditional blanket. Twenty minutes later, having spent its wrath, the storm moved on to dissipate over the South African countryside to the west. Shafts of brilliant light snuck through the clouds and glistened off a land buried beneath an inch of ice marbles.

The village men and I returned to their fields, afraid of what we might find. Their faces fell. Maize fields that could have fed their families for months had been pummeled to nothing more than splintered stalks pointing skyward, a lumpy green pulp of leaves and unfilled cobs lying in a slurry of ice and mud at their base. Inside my gut clenched a heavy emptiness, knowing how much had been lost.

Back in the rondavel, the party was over. People talked in hushed tones about the devastation outside. I thought it might be time to explore this new mystery, hail doctors, so I asked one of the men. He told me that some traditional faith healers, the folks who cast bones, beat drums and mix potions, claim an ability to fend off hail storms. They reroute them elsewhere to protect their own villagers' crops. Competing hail doctors occasionally make a contest out of it, threatening to send hail to each other's village.

In addition to throwing bones, chanting and other spell casting methods, two special techniques can be used against hail. Skyrockets are sometimes used to create a percussive clap at the base of the clouds, scaring the storm away. Some hail doctors build giant pyres of wood and trash to send up plumes of soot-laden smoke as a storm nears. Remarkably, both methods contain a kernel of science. Either could bring moisture out of the clouds as water, not ice. Households they "protect" pay their hail doctors with live chickens and other tributes. The more successful hail doctors eat well. Today's damage, however, would require an explanation and some serious discussions whenever the doctor could be found.

After a bit, the roads dried enough to be passable and we set out for home. Following the track back toward the highway, I noticed, off to one side, a group of men. They were armed with sticks and clubs, silently walking in single file along a path that led toward that lone rondavel on the village edge. I shuddered. Sitting beside me, my wife pointed, muttering,

"Uh-oh." When we passed that home, those once-white bed linens lay in tattered wads in the mud in front of the lady's rondavel. It was pretty obvious what was about to happen. My stomach tightened. This was tribal, rooted in hundreds of years of Sotho culture. I did not understand the origins or the reasons, and I certainly would not be welcome to get involved. I kept driving.

The next week I asked Manapo what happened to the woman. My curiosity was probably tactless. She was silent a long time. My question caught her between two cultures, two ways of seeing the world, two widely divergent value systems. All she would say before changing the subject was, "She lived."

The Walls Have Ears

Invite the boss to lunch? What a great idea. A little gustatory rapport building between a leader in the Ministry of Agriculture and our USAID-CSU project. Why not?

Several reasons came to mind. For one, people in my position just did not do this. People on contracted project teams, the "blue passport" types, did not invite their host country boss to lunch. Especially not the number two man in the Ministry. If I had been a US government employee with an "official" maroon passport, it might have been different. For bona fide State Department diplomats with their black passports, no problem. But for we contract hires, who rank only one step above the Peace Corps in the U.S. in-country hierarchy, protocol demanded deference, not conviviality. To hell with protocol.

Or maybe I should forget this plan because some official embassy Americans might resent my direct, intimate access to local power? But they already did, even before this lunch idea. I usually sat on the Ministry's side of the table in negotiations with USAID even though the latter funded my project and paid my salary. In the vernacular of the day, my job was "institution building." I took that to mean strengthening the capabilities of local Ministry of Agriculture officials. If that meant teaching them how to drive a hard bargain with the donors, then so be it.

121

Sometimes a project comes out of Washington that fits poorly with the host country culture or politics or the economic realities in the field. Then the local officials may need someone to help defend their culture, their dreams or just their way of doing business. In Lesotho, I was that guy, and this rankled some of the maroon passport types. One or two smirked that I had "gone native," implying that I no longer represented American interests very well. I also heard indirectly of the occasional cocktail party discussion on how to "rein in Eckert." To me, it was all great fun. What it meant was I had become a partial insider with our Basotho colleagues, just exactly where I needed to be for maximum effectiveness.

Finally, maybe my Ministry of Agriculture boss should worry about being seen lunching with me. He, too, might face scrutiny and suspicion within his highly politicized culture if he hobnobbed too frequently with foreigners. Would I get him into trouble?

It boiled down to a budding friendship between two colleagues from very different points on the human spectrum. Lunch could be enjoyable, even productive. If nurtured, this friendship might sustain our complex project and deepen its potential. It might, in fact, be essential.

Just down the street from the Ministry stood the Maseru Club, a tree-lined tennis venue left over from the days of British rule. Its quiet, discreet veranda and semi-decent lunch menu beckoned. I asked Chaka Ntsane, Deputy Permanent Secretary of Agriculture, to lunch and he accepted.

Chaka was unique. Westernized when he needed to be, yet steeped in Sesotho culture, he moved freely and with influence through the multi-cultural maze of characters, programs and competing policies that comprised foreign assistance in Lesotho in the late 1970s. He was also a raconteur, a bon vivant, and a politician on his way up.

* * *

After WWII, the U.S. Marshall Plan spent $13 billion reconstructing and equipping Europe to raise it from the ashes. The dramatic "Flowering of Europe" led, naively, to the idea that money and the latest technology would bring similar results in under developed nations. And so, foreign assistance was born, directed at under-developed countries. What no one recognized at the time was that Europe flourished, not because of our money and machines, nor our ideas and advice, but because the education, skills, and attitudes of Europe's people remained intact, only needing something tangible to work with. Also, the war had destroyed most of the entrenched institutional barriers to expression and creativity, unleashing the energies of millions.

In the ensuing decades, U.S. foreign assistance to under-developed nations labored on, producing a checkered, often undistinguished history. Rarely were projects clearly successful even in the short run and often they showed little impact over the long haul. Occasionally they failed outright. Monies were spent without much accountability. End of project evaluations were a joke. It was, after all, the Cold War and the West was locked in competition with a hostile Soviet Bloc. Seducing the allegiance of nonaligned nations became a core policy goal. We threw money, training, infrastructure, and weapons at them hoping to bring them into our camp, ultimately making them dependent on the West instead of the

Soviets. We never used the word "neocolonialism," but in actual fact we were damn good at it.

Developing countries played the same game but for different reasons. Donor money built offices and infrastructure, which local politicians bragged about to their constituencies. Vehicles, computers and other modern imported goods arrived to add bling to government offices. Education and training ranked high on the list of project goodies. In developing nations, salaried jobs were so scarce that degree credentials and training certificates became screening tools for employment and promotion, whether the skills related to the job or not. Donor money funded massive amounts of training and academic degrees, especially if project goals included institution building. Donor money also funded international travel to overseas conferences, short courses, observation tours, contract negotiations and more. Per diem and allowances collected during travel abroad could, in a matter of a few weeks, equal half a year's salary for an African civil servant back home. People lusted after chances for official travel. One of our local counterparts was so busy traveling and collecting per diem that she was rarely at her desk.

In Lesotho, another dynamic also played a role. Assistance to this tiny nonstrategic nation could be trumpeted by the donors as helping to fight apartheid in the surrounding South Africa. Donors of all stripes competed with each other to do so. Here, in one of the smallest, least strategic countries in Africa, more than 70 nations and assistance agencies came to biennial donors' conferences, laying out an array of proposals, a shopping list for the Government of Lesotho. In 1977, when our project arrived, the country was relatively poor and there were no millionaires. But a year earlier, to assist in the anti-apartheid fight, the United Nations Development Programme had written a fist full of checks for dozens of projects, many of which were little more than a title and a wild idea sketched out on a scrap of paper. Abilities to manage these monies were paper thin and accountability almost nonexistent. When we left in 1980, there were several millionaires.

* * *

Chaka, however, was committed to making our LASA project different, as were all six of us from Colorado State University. We wanted to use the project to bridge gaps between our nations, between our cultures, between our bureaucracies. We sought to be friends with our Basotho colleagues first, to set a firm grounding for collaboration. As friendships grew, so did the trust we shared. Lunch at the Maseru Club was just another building block as far as I was concerned.

Our first lunch took place shortly after a certain British horticulturalist had ended his tour, prematurely it seemed to me, and left the country, embittered by his project's inability to get anything done. I knew him, but not well. We both led projects in the Ministry of Agriculture and infrequently met at staff meetings. Soon after our arrival, my wife, Betty, and I joined a small dinner party in this man's home. We were shocked to hear a very negative anti-Basotho tone in the conversation that night. Assuming privacy within their own house, and assisted by much gin and tonic, our hosts and some other guests, mostly Brits, offered a steady barrage of

125

disparaging comments about "the locals," their strange habits, their limited intelligence, and their untrustworthiness.

I said almost nothing at table that night and we never went back. However, by chance, immediately after this Englishman left, Betty and I were assigned his house. Large by local standards, the Prime Minister kept this residence in his official housing pool for special allocations. It sat behind walls on a one acre lot shaded by eucalyptus and pine trees. Under this canopy the horticulturalist and his wife had created a verdant, flower filled microclimate where new pines sprouted from fallen seed, tranquility filled the evening and the rroou - rroou of rock pigeons woke us in the morning. This special house came up during lunch that day.

"Say, Chaka," I began, "I want to thank you for the house. I know you had something to do with it; I saw your name on the paperwork." We had already started using our giant living room to entertain dignitaries. Diplomats and high level government officers seemed comfortable there with us and Mr. and Mrs. Chaka Ntsane had been among our first guests.

He smiled. "You know my wife, Theresa, controls the Prime Minister's housing pool. I just thought that my American project leader needed a better residence than that tiny place we gave you when you arrived."

"Well, it sure is beautiful," I said. "That Brit did a really bang-up job with the landscaping. But you know, Betty and I were over there for dinner one night and we were shocked. He really didn't like the people or much of anything else here. If people like that are going to be so negative, then they ought not to represent their countries." Chaka was quiet and the conversation turned elsewhere.

In Sesotho culture, as with many others, people visiting each other often save the most important topic for last. One may talk all night over dinner and drinks with an African friend, only to have the main reason for the evening revealed at the door or in the driveway as everyone says good night. This was one such case. At the end of our lunch, we sat there nursing coffees on the veranda waiting for our bill and listening to the sounds of the afternoon measured out by the thuk - tuk. . thuk - tuk of a single tennis match. Chaka returned to the topic of the British horticulturalist.

"Jerry, I have to tell you something. And I want you to make sure your team also understands this clearly." He paused. I turned toward him. This was serious.

"That British horticulturalist? He left because we cancelled his work permit and did not renew his project. We knew how he felt and what he was saying. We don't have to work with people like that. This is our country. We are a sensitive people. If you speak badly of us, we will know. You must always remember that the walls have ears."

I was not surprised. I had seen Americans in Pakistan lose their influence with the Pakistanis because their own negative attitudes showed. With our team in Lesotho, there would not be a problem. We all liked our hosts. We found their culture fascinating and were each forming friendships with our Basotho colleagues. Nonetheless, I passed on Chaka's strong words of caution to the Colorado State team in our next staff meeting.

But I got to thinking about the walls having ears. Was Chaka saying that our houses were bugged? Team members all lived in housing provided by the government. Installing listening devices before we moved in would have been easy.

No, that didn't seem the right answer. They would have needed imported surveillance gear, skilled technicians to install it and people paid to listen to our conversations. Too expensive for an agricultural project of no strategic, diplomatic, or intelligence value.

Was Chaka just using allegory to make his point? Certainly disparaging, denigrating attitudes, held strongly enough to be spoken out loud at home, could color daily exchanges at the office as well. Voice tone, body language, location of meetings, choice of words; there exist a thousand ways someone's disdain for others might slip out.

Pakistan taught me the intelligence value of office trash. I had no indications that the Government of Lesotho was reading our trash in Maseru. But on those rare occasions when I wrote something confidential, either to my embassy or to contacts in the South African Prime Minister's office across the border, all the drafts went home with me to our backyard incinerator where I personally stirred the ashes into chaff.

Then I remembered the servants, the ever-present servants. They might not be in the room, but they could be right around the corner in the kitchen, or mixing with the crowd serving food or cocktails. A good servant works quietly, inconspicuously, efficiently nearby. If they spoke English, they heard most everything. And most everything could be a lot. In the privacy of their own homes, after a couple of stiff drinks of commissary tax-free liquor, people can let their guard down. Americans will assume their home is their private lair just like back in the States, that the outside world is excluded, that what happens inside stays inside. For those with loose tongues, this can be disastrous.

The servant possibility has another wrinkle. We expats generally paid our servants poorly, mirroring the local wage, yet internally rejoicing in the rock bottom cost of household skills. In Lesotho, for example, Neheng, our maid, cook, and babysitter received a single room, food from our kitchen when she wanted and less than $2 a day in cash. But I never questioned her loyalty. She was like family, essentially living with us in her tiny room just outside the kitchen. We were loyal to each other. She honored me with the Sesotho name *Ra Thabong*, "father of happiness," and gave her new baby the middle name Jerry. Thebua Jerry Hlasoa. I liked that.

In Pakistan, however, intelligence is a highly refined art and the game plan might have played out differently. In Lahore a decade earlier, I supported six indoor servants and most of their 49 family dependents for a total monthly cost of $120. The tri-lingual cook, our highest paid employee, received one dollar per ten-hour day with two meals but no lodging. The day watchman/gardener received $0.40 for his eight hour day. Looking back, I wonder how they lived on that, yet millions of rural residents lived on $0.10 a day. How easy would it have been for Pakistan's Inter-Services Intelligence agency to find servants in key households who, for a small wage top-up, would report to their handlers what they overheard at their jobs?

I also remembered Simone, our family's cook and maid for the two years we lived in Meudon, France in 1948-49. Dad worked for the Marshall Plan as an agricultural expert. Like a big sister, Simone helped Mom look after us children as part of her regular duties. One day I came home from school to find Simone gone. American Embassy security officers had ordered Dad to fire her, only a month before our tour was up.

Presumably she had attended a meeting or maybe even held a membership card in the French Communist Party. In those days, Dad carried a black passport so Simone's politics mattered, at least to the embassy security guys. Maybe Simone was the ears on our walls in Meudon, but I seriously doubt it. Besides, as a fifth grader, I didn't even know what a communist party was. What I did know was that Simone cooked wonderful artichokes, *biftek au buerre* and *chocolat mousse*. I remember when she left how unfair I thought all this cloak and dagger stuff was.

I believe that Chaka was only metaphorically driving his point home. In all my years overseas, I'm pretty sure no one ever bugged any of my houses but then I never really looked either. With one or two question marks in Pakistan, our servants were all loyal and trusted. But the Basotho people *are* quite sensitive to how outsiders perceive them. Also overseas Americans are a diverse lot, just like they are at home, and within that diversity are some insensitive, callous individuals who think they are somehow "better." Whether we recognize it or not, our culture can include an assumed pre-eminence, an arrogance, which is hard to overcome, especially when we don't understand the local people and their cultures well.

The answer, however, is simple. Learn your hosts' lifeways and cultures to the point where you can see them as valid given their circumstances, where you can appreciate the origins and rationale of what happens around you, and in that light respect or even admire your local colleagues. With that foundation, you are unlikely to say something you might regret. And then, it doesn't matter if the walls have ears or not.

"If I Have Served My People - - -"

The phone rang first thing Monday morning in the International Programs Office at Colorado State University. My wife, Betty, the office administrator, took the call. After a moment's silence, Betty called urgently across the cubicles, "Jerry! Get on the phone." I grabbed the receiver and into our morning, with the hollow metallic resonance of an international connection, flooded the weeping voice of Julia Ntsekhe, our good friend, calling from Lesotho.

"They killed Manapo. They took Manapo and her husband and that other minister and his wife up on the mountain road and they just shot them." Julia paused to get her voice under control. Betty and I, stunned into silence, groped for our own thoughts. Not our Manapo. Not our sweet friend, my student, our boss, the mother of our godchild. Not Manapo!

Julia couldn't say much. The news was fresh, still fragmentary. She hesitated to give details over the phone. In Lesotho, the walls do sometimes have ears as Chaka had warned me and one never knows who's listening. Political killings spread fear and silence quickly. I hung up and bolted for our local newspaper office with its wire service connections. I was numb, focused only on navigating safely across town.

* * *

Associated Press: November 16, 1986, AM cycle

Former Lesotho Cabinet Ministers Reported Shot Dead

JOHANNESBURG:. Two former ministers of the deposed Lesotho Prime Minister Leabua Jonathan's government were among five people abducted and shot to death in that tiny mountain kingdom, the South African Press Association reported Sunday. In a dispatch from its reporter in Lesotho, the news agency quoted a relative of one of the ex-ministers as saying the two men and their wives were at a friend's home ... when gunmen abducted them at 11 p.m. Saturday. The captives were driven into the Maluti Mountains and shot, the agency said, quoting the relative. The news agency identified the victims as Desmond Sixishe, former minister of information and Vincent Makhele, former foreign minister and their wives.

Those last three words made it real. Manapo was Mrs. Desmond Sixishe. Later as I learned more details, my grief turned to anger, then revulsion. The full truth would poison my life-long romance with Africa. I had loved Africa, blindly perhaps, but I loved her nonetheless. Many people do. My naiveté died with Manapo, suddenly, discarded in a ditch beside an unpaved mountain road. At that moment, all I knew was an inner emptiness. "Damn it! Damn it!" I had warned her that this might happen. Had I not been insistent enough? Could I have changed her fate?

Even as I formed the question, I knew the answer. Manapo's life was well beyond my influence or control, her destiny fixed before we ever met. Like two passing comets, our time together was all too brief before her trajectory took her onward, as did mine; hers toward a footnote in history and mine to be her witness. I spent the rest of the morning doing the only thing left to me. I wrote an impassioned eulogy and gave copies to every faculty member and graduate student in our department and across campus that had called her friend. There were many.

* * *

I first met Manapo ten years earlier. Colorado State University won a U.S. government contract for an agricultural planning project in Lesotho. My department chair and I flew over for a week to negotiate final project details. I would lead the university's field team. As head of the Ministry of Agriculture's Planning Unit, Manapo was my designated counterpart, in-country she would be my boss.

At the arrivals lounge, she greeted us with *"Khotso, Ntate,"* a respectful "Peace, Father. Welcome to Lesotho." Her broad smile put us at ease. She was light skinned for an African, her hair done in a short Afro. Others welcomed us enthusiastically as well, but I noticed that they deferred to Manapo's lead in the conversation. Her last name, Moshoeshoe, matched that of His Majesty, King Moshoeshoe II, and I made a mental note to explore that linkage later. We chatted about nothing much as strangers will do when they first meet; our long trip over, the lack of rain this winter, the coal-smoke cloud over the capital city of Maseru. We scheduled our first formal meeting, said goodbye and someone from the American embassy whisked us off to the Lesotho Hilton.

As we got down to business during the week, Manapo and I quickly found common ground. We both were committed that "our" project would differ from the norm.

Two decades of America's agricultural foreign assistance had produced more failed projects than successes. This we would change. Between us we came up with two completely new project strategies.

"Why don't we reverse the normal project sequence?" I suggested. "Why don't those of you who will be our counterparts here in Maseru come to CSU first, get your degrees and we will delay the in-country phase until later? Then we can work together more as equals than as advisers and advisees." She bought this idea immediately. USAID started amending the project time line.

Then Manapo came up with a novel idea of her own. "As long as we are going to be in Colorado for a year, could we have a seminar where we students explain our country to your professors? And can it be required for everyone who is coming over here to live?"

"If I organize the seminar, can you organize the content?" I asked.

"Of course, Ntate."

It worked. Manapo was a knowledgeable and passionate teacher. We met weekly for most of the year the Basotho were on campus studying for their MA degrees. By the time our team arrived in Maseru, we Americans were more in tune with our host nation, its people, politics and culture, than most diplomats who had been there for years. Together we set out to build a modern planning and policy analysis division within the Ministry of Agriculture.

Something else about Manapo struck me. Those eight years in Pakistan had provided my first real exposure to a developing country. With nothing to compare it to, I really hadn't noticed the near total exclusion of women from government service. In Muslim Pakistan, the secretarial and clerical staff, the janitors, office administrators, and certainly the managers were all men. Even when you shared a meal at a colleague's home, the women remained out of sight in the kitchen.

Here in Lesotho, however, women seemed to be everywhere. They looked you right in the eye, spoke to men as equals, headed high offices in government and made decisions on their own. Most of Lesotho's men worked across the border in South Africa. As a result, women headed seventy percent of Lesotho's households and dominated the middle ranks of government.

Manapo exemplified the Mosotho woman: confident, out-spoken, both educated and street smart. Others sought her leadership, deferred to her judgment. Not only was she competent and experienced, she had a woman's sensitivity to the human side of her administrative decisions. Later I would learn of another reason she led so easily, her membership in the royal family. Both the king and the prime minister were close relatives. For now, I simply marveled at a woman calling the shots for an entire government, beginning her sentences with, "I want this project to do ..." or "You will be responsible for ..." What a change southern Africa would be from South Asia.

The first several months went well. Americans and Basotho both worked hard to build an effective team. After our year together at CSU, we brought our team rapport with us to Lesotho. We socialized with each other, another novel departure from standard foreign assistance practice. Our research began in earnest. In a nation with no reliable data, our first job was to build a statistical picture of Lesotho's economy and its farm sector. To help gather the data, I was slowly building working relationships with economists and policy analysts across the border in South Africa, mostly beneath the radar.

Manapo and I agreed that Lesotho's economic future depended critically on continued employment for Basotho men across the border in South Africa. Lesotho had almost no private sector jobs at that time. Except for those few in government service, nearly every able-bodied man worked in South Africa, mostly in gold or coal mining or in trucking. Access to mining jobs was tightly controlled in Pretoria. No one in Maseru really knew how much longer those jobs would remain available and because of Lesotho's vehement anti-apartheid stance, their government refused to even talk to the South Africans. Yet, someone had to.

Why not go up to Pretoria, I thought, use my white, foreign, academic status to get in the door, and ask South Africa's policy makers how they viewed the future need for workers from Lesotho? I was young, probably naive. Nobody told me this was not how it was done, that there were protocols to be followed. So I called a man in Pretoria who I had never met but whose job title said Director of Planning. To my complete surprise he said "Sure, come on up." Dawie Mullins had only recently obtained his doctorate in economics. His dissertation research on the country's economy was so accurate that the powers in Pretoria classified it, locked up all the copies and offered Dawie a job in the Office of the Economic Advisor to the Prime Minister. Dawie was young, committed and enthusiastic. Perhaps he also did not yet know how things were "supposed'" to be done.

With Manapo's approval I drove to Pretoria, where I spent three days being briefed at the highest levels about labor issues affecting Lesotho. A stranger, me, with no official credentials, a citizen from a foreign country that officially rejected South African apartheid, wandering in off the street and asking pointed questions about policies and plans governing sensitive relations between two fiercely bickering nations. The sheer implausibility of it all was dumbfounding. Yet the Economic Advisor's office opened its doors and answered my questions candidly. The trust and friendship built that week allowed Dawie and I to work together for more than a decade. In the end, we would help to redirect his country's economic and racial policies, irrevocably speeding the end of apartheid.

To this day, I do not know what role Simon Brand played in Dawie's open response to my phone call requesting an appointment. Or for that matter, in my acceptance by South Africa's policy establishment for years thereafter. In 1962-63, Simon and I had been Masters Degree students together in Stanford's Food Research Institute. We became good friends, Simon and his wife, Ina, invited me to dinner occasionally. Sometimes, late at night when studies had fried our brains, Simon and I would repair to Tressider Student Union for an hour of intense ping-pong. Now, fifteen years later, Simon had emerged as Economic Advisor to the Prime Minister in South Africa, giving him a seminal influence on South Africa's policies, in both economics and other spheres.

In this first encounter with Dawie, while reading the materials they gave me, I noticed a data point that didn't seem quite right, an assumed link between jobs and economic growth. The more I read, the more critical that one number became. It seemed about twice too large, and much of South Africa's future employment planning pivoted squarely on this single fulcrum. A few days later I wrote Dawie pointing out what I felt was a flaw. Dawie concurred. Their model and its implications changed. Projections and policies were adjusted. Our collaboration was off and running. All, as I say, under the radar, because the U.S. government was paying for me to help Lesotho, not South Africa. Lesotho had become a rallying point in the anti-apartheid movement, serving occasionally as base for guerrilla incursions mounted by the armed wing of the ANC. I suppose my actions could be viewed as aiding the enemy. However, Manapo and I both felt that helping South Africa employ more Basotho was helping Lesotho very directly since there were so few domestic jobs available.

Lesotho and South Africa had very few diplomatic or even administrative ties in those days. Lesotho simply refused to deal with the hated apartheid regime. This created a communications breach into which Manapo and I were unwittingly drawn.

As part of my job, I traveled to Pretoria from time to time for "technical discussions," gathering information (or was it intelligence?) that would help Lesotho plan systematically. I kept Manapo fully briefed and after informing her uncle, Prime Minister Leabua Jonathon, she approved these contacts. Occasionally I worked with one of Dawie's colleagues, Dr. Piet du Toit, Director of Policy in the Economic Advisor's Office. We built a comfortable working trust. About 18 months into my tour in Maseru, Piet came to Lesotho on a tourist visa. My wife and I invited him to our house for dinner and a glass or two of South Africa's best red wine in front of our fireplace.

True to the southern African culture, Piet saved his most important discussion topic for last. As our evening wore down, he came 'round to his real point.

"Jerry, my Prime Minister wants to get a confidential message to your Prime Minister Jonathon. Do you know of any way that I might do that?"

Of course I did. Piet must have known that already. Suddenly this was no longer a "tourist" visit. By now, Manapo and I were as close as working colleagues can be. I called her *Ausi*, or sister. She referred to me as *Abuti*, her brother. She was one of Lesotho's best and brightest, a civil servant rapidly rising toward greater contributions. While she carried the royal surname, Moshoeshoe, she was also Leabua Jonathon's niece. Between her government job and her family contacts, she and Jonathon undoubtedly spoke often.

"Sure, I can do that for you." I thought it was a one-time request.

The next day I met privately with Manapo to explain Piet's message, something to do with sharing trade and customs revenues between the two nations. This innocuous topic was probably a test, to see if this back channel could work. A day or two later, Jonathon sent a positive response, again through Manapo, to me, then to Piet. A line of communication had opened just a crack between two estranged nations. Sharing in this small success brought Manapo and me a little closer as colleagues.

As the Ministry of Agriculture's Chief Planning Officer, Manapo wanted to devote her Masters thesis research to exploring alternative planning methods that she might apply in Lesotho. Together we searched out literature on several other African nations with their five-year plans, their 20-year perspective plans, and their national consensus building exercises. We wanted to visit nearby Gaborone, the nearby capital of Botswana, to study their widely acclaimed success, but Manapo's boss declared Botswana off limits. Even though the outside world touted the Botswana case study, our bosses felt there were too many expatriates running the show in Gaborone. We were told it was "not a proper 'African' example – Lesotho has nothing to learn from them."

The only other success story within driving distance was Pretoria. And, whether their politics let the Basotho admit it or not, decisions taken in South Africa governed every aspect of daily lives in Lesotho. Coordination with Pretoria could be critical for a Chief Planning Officer like Manapo. Hesitantly, Manapo asked if there were any way she could go up to Pretoria and study their long-term planning system like I seemed able to do. Maybe the academic nature of her thesis research would make it OK, she suggested. I called Dawie, who cleared the idea within his boss, Simon Brand. Manapo cleared it with her uncle, Prime Minister Leabua Jonathon. Without further fanfare, we quietly launched a novel consultation between these two countries.

I decided to drive to Pretoria in our project's Chevy Blazer. It was a scenic drive of four or five hours through rolling countryside of large farms growing corn and alfalfa, dotted with cows. Not too different from Iowa or parts of Nebraska, except that the farm labor was invariably black. Manapo invited her deputy, Mrs. Matseiea Morojele along, partly because it made practical sense and partly for appearances. As we prepared to depart, both of them climbed into the Blazer's back seat.

"Hey. At least one of you should sit up here with me so we can talk," I protested. That's when I learned another wrinkle of the local culture that characterized apartheid.

"Ntate," Manapo said, "We are going to drive just now through the Orange Free State. That countryside is filled with Afrikaners and apartheid is still very much alive over there. If they see us sitting in front with you, they will think we are — what's the right word — your concubines. If we sit in back, they will think nothing of it because that's where their servants sit."

"If I sit here driving, with my two bosses riding in the back, that will make me the chauffeur, right?" I grinned. They saw the humor in that, but they rode to Pretoria in the back seat nonetheless.

The visit went well. Official South Africa welcomed Manapo and Matseiea with the deference and status usually reserved for visiting diplomats. They met with senior specialists and policy analysts. Manapo asked direct, penetrating questions. For the present she saw two nations that needed dialogue with each other. In the future, she imagined a mutually beneficial, cross-border cooperation and she wondered why that couldn't begin soon. The South Africans were candid. We extended our visit half a day to squeeze in some last minute meetings with top officials who wanted to meet these remarkable women. One or two of their briefings reached levels of confidentiality that excluded me, which was fine. There comes a time when the facilitator should back out and let a new dynamic proceed without him.

Before we left for home, I thought we might have some fun. I asked the women if they would like to help integrate a local restaurant and they both said Yes. In those days, South Africa had begun relaxing the rules of apartheid one tiny step at a time, an incremental approach that could be reversed if all Hell broke out. In one of those steps, legally mandated hotel and restaurant segregation had been replaced with local choice. Hotels could, if they wanted, get themselves classified as "international" and accept clients of all colors. The three of us were staying at the internationalized Pretoria Holiday Inn. Just around the corner stood an upscale steak house offering a quality executive lunch. Before suggesting this adventure, I talked to the white owner and manager who welcomed the idea of becoming an "international restaurant."

My friends would be his first-ever black customers.

We arrived straight from the Prime Minister's offices, still power dressed in business suits. Matseiea wore her hair in cornrows; Manapo sported a short-cropped Afro. Subtle gold jewelry suggested upper-class, educated, business women. The manager pushed his waiter aside, grabbed some menus, draped a linen napkin over his arm, and with the flair of a maitre d'hotel, escorted us to a prominent table. Wide-eyed Afrikaners watched our little procession. He pulled each woman's chair back, sat them gracefully, and with proper protocol, handed them their menus from the left, with his left hand. A few polite words about his daily menu special, a hint of a bow, and he left us to ponder our choices.

Watching our host slide chairs beneath Manapo and Matseiea brought a sudden realization. Not 500 yards from this restaurant lay a well-manicured city park. In that park were benches carefully stenciled with "*Blankies*" and "*Nie Blankies*," Whites and Non-Whites in Afrikaans. That public park had not yet been "internationalized." My comfortably seated friends could be arrested just 500 yards away from here for choosing to sit on the wrong park bench. I was about to mention this anachronism when one puffy, ruddy-faced Afrikaner couple seated nearby stood up in a huff, grabbed their frightened child and stalked out. Their appetizers lay unfinished. Matseiea was nervous. Manapo just smiled.

Liquor laws formed another oddity during South Africa's long-overdue journey into the 20th Century. Establishments with liquor licenses were generally either the high-toned or the dives. In everyday restaurants and steak houses, it was hard to buy wine or beer with your meal. Rather than change the law to let restaurants sell alcohol openly, the rules makers invented a cumbersome system that allowed restaurants to open and serve wine or beer but only if customers brought it with them.

Today, after the manager took our meal orders, he leaned over next to my ear and whispered, "Did you bring a wine?" I hadn't even thought of it and told him so. "I will take care of it," he whispered. Then he stood erect and announced in a voice loud enough to be heard several tables away, "I will fetch your wine for you. Just now, sir." He stressed the word "your" ever so slightly. What appeared at our table was one of South Africa's finest vintages, a 10-year old Pinotage from a highly acclaimed vineyard near Capetown, straight from the restaurant owner's private stock. He proudly showed me the label, uncorked the bottle, let me sniff the cork, and then poured for the women, over their right shoulders of course. Very proper. All with his own conspiratorial smile. A perfect meal followed, neatly rounding off a memorable trip to Pretoria. Pleasantly mellowed with all this great wine, good food and flamboyant hospitality, we headed back through the international parking lot to our international hotel. There was laughter in Manapo's voice when I heard her say, "That ought to give those Afrikaners something to talk about tonight."

*　*　*

Manapo seemed happy, even effervescent at times. Her life was on track. She was living her dreams. Her country needed her and she met that need with sensitive yet definitive action at the top of government. One day, toward the end of our three years in Lesotho, she came into my office unannounced.

"Jerry, there is something I want to show you. Someone I want you to meet."

"OK." I was always ready to bend to her schedule. "How 'bout now?"

"No. It has to be someplace private. Out of town. This is just for you and Betty."

I suggested a quiet lunch at one of my favorite hideaways, the isolated Blue Mountain Inn with its grass-thatched roof and its staff well trained by British colonialists, some 20 miles down the road. "My treat," I offered.

Betty and I arrived a few minutes early. The room was empty, which was good. I talked to the management to ensure their discrete attention. Manapo came a bit late, dressed in her finest. She beamed a smile as broad as all Africa. With her was a handsome man, a few years her senior, wearing the crisp black suit and white silk tie of an important politician. My wife's first impression was "My Gawd. Look at that gorgeous hunk."

"Betty, Jerry. I would like you to meet Desmond Sixishe." Her excitement was barely controlled.

We shook hands all around. "Manapo. *Ausi.* Sister. You should know me better by now." I knew that hardly any Mosotho used his or her English name when with friends. Those names raise uncomfortable colonial shadows.

I turned to Desmond. "Most southern Africans have both an English and a local name. Don't you? And may I use the latter?" He smiled broadly, the ice now broken. "Tsepo. Yes, please call me Tsepo."

We shared a good meal. The service was impeccable. Tsepo bought a nice bottle of Pinotage, South Africa's signature contribution to wine lovers everywhere.

"Bad politics should not keep us from enjoying good wine," announced Tsepo. Our laughter and chatter filled the small dining room. Manapo bubbled, obviously in love. Neither Betty nor I had seen this sparkle in her eyes before. In a very Western gesture, she laid her hand gently on his, in plain sight for us to see.

Toward the end of our lengthy lunch, however, something began to nag at me. Maybe I was being over-protective of my "sister." However, the more he talked, the more Tsepo seemed ever-so-slightly too smooth. Parts of him lay beneath a veneer I couldn't penetrate. His smile, his polished words, hinted, if only barely, at secrets. Besides, the shape of his face, his very dark complexion, and his surname told me he wasn't Mosotho. Bluntly candid as usual, I asked, and confirmed — he was Xhosa, the dominant tribe in the Transkei homeland of South Africa. That seemed odd. Why was a slick Xhosa politician hovering around one of the most influential women in Lesotho's government?

The next day I made an excuse to visit the American Embassy, found a good friend with top diplomatic clearances, and closed his door for a chat.

"Who is this Tsepo Desmond Sixishe anyway?" I knew that I was wading in well beyond my security clearance level. "And why is he hobnobbing with Lesotho's Cabinet? He is a Xhosa, for God's sake. Basotho distrust the Xhosa – deeply. Everyone knows that. They consider the Xhosa devious, too aggressive."

My friend took a slow deep breath. "Off the record? You didn't hear it from me, OK?" Ground rules I had already assumed because we had done this before on other topics. He continued.

"This Sixishe guy is doing something for Leabua Jonathon's office that requires visiting communist countries in the Soviet Union. We aren't sure what just yet but we are tracking his travel. We can't figure why Lesotho sends Mr. Sixishe to places like Albania and Cuba, but we don't like it."

We chatted a bit about the Soviet Union's thinly veiled attempts to destabilize this part of the world. It was no secret that they supported the liberation movement's armed struggle with guns, training and money. With Soviet influence in Mozambique on the east coast, and a Cuban military presence in Angola on the west, it looked very much like a pincer movement cutting South Africa off from contact with the rest of the continent to the north. How Lesotho fit into the larger scheme, if it did at all, was unclear. But, being located wholly within South Africa, a communist-leaning Lesotho could undermine the whole region's stability. My friend summed up his answer to my question.

"What Sixishe's exact role is," he continued, "we just don't know yet. But we are pretty sure he's up to no good." Then with emphasis, as though it were an order, "Steer clear of that guy, Jerry. He is probably dangerous. Steer *very* clear."

Overnight, I weighed my options with this bit of intelligence. For leaking Embassy secrets, I could be fired, my project disgraced. Yet Ausi Manapo was, I feared, at risk. Reluctantly, I made a choice. I found her in her office just before noon the next day. I waited in the back until she showed her last official visitor out. She closed the door, broke out her sandwich and leaned back in her chair. "What's on your mind, Abuti?"

This would not be an easy conversation. How do you tell a 32-year old woman that the person she loves might be a threat? And that I had spied on him. What would happen to her sparkle? And, not the least of my worries, could what I had to say, what I had done, damage our personal relationship? I threw everything I had into my preamble in order to cushion what was coming. I told her how precious our friendship was, how much I loved her as my *Ausi*, as my colleague. I built the case that she was critical to her country's emerging future. But then I had to tell her, without disclosing my source, that Tsepo bothered me. And I gave her just enough of the "why" to anchor the point. She was gracious. We were still friends. Then, she spoke candidly.

"Jerry, I know there are risks. There are always risks in this environment. Especially when I work where I do in my government. We are surrounded by an enemy, by apartheid, by an armed struggle for liberation. Just last month, you must have heard the machine guns down by the border below your house. It is dangerous for all of us here, even for you. You know that, *Abuti*."

Then she softened. "However, *Abuti*, I have found my life's love. I want to marry Tsepo and I want us to have children, lots of children, and a house. Please understand how important this is to me and wish us the best."

I felt I had to escalate my plea just one notch, one last desperate try.

"*Ausi*? Please? Let me say one more thing. Then I will shut up and wish you the best of happiness. Manapo, my dear friend. I am so afraid that if you marry Tsepo, you could get hurt. He is dangerous. Even my embassy thinks so. While you may be trying to serve your people, he could lead you into a situation where you could end up in front of a firing squad."

She paused. She had heard me. Her eyes steadied into a seriousness that I remember as though it were yesterday. Then she said, "If that happens – if I do end up in front of a firing squad . . ." Again she paused, choosing her words carefully. "If when I stand there, I know that it is because I have served my people – then that will just be the way it ends." She turned and looked silently at something in the distance beyond her window. Her future? Perhaps.

In the end, it wasn't the apartheid struggle that killed Manapo. Nor was it the broader East-West cold war confrontation in which the big powers used small African nations as pawns or surrogates. Manapo was just another casualty of the heinous coup and counter-coup merry-go-round that all too often defines African politics.

Tsepo Desmond Sixishe lost his job as Minister of Information when Leabua was deposed, as did his buddy, the Foreign Minister. The two of them must have been plotting yet another overthrow. Perhaps Tsepo planned on getting help from his friends in Cuba or the Soviet bloc – we will never know. Someone, however, was worried and putting these two schemers under house arrest would not suffice. When the case went to trial years later, the court convicted two of the King's cousins of ordering the killings.

The gunmen came for the two ex-ministers during a private dinner party in the university town of Roma. They wore military camouflage fatigues and masks. Unfortunately, Manapo knew and befriended nearly everyone in town. She recognized one of them behind his mask and spoke to him by name. She begged him to spare her husband for their children's sake. It backfired. Knowing they had been identified, the gunmen decided to leave no witnesses and grabbed the wives as well. The one survivor, the hostess of the evening, was Manapo's sister who escaped, gravely wounded, through the kitchen door into the night. News travels fast, especially among the elite in Africa. Julia Ntsekhe's tearful phone call reached us the following Monday morning.

Africa Weeping

Our small plane banked into its landing approach to Maseru, Lesotho. I watched from the window as the distance between the plane and the looming rock face ahead closed rapidly. The old Maseru International Airport offered passengers a rare treat. The runway headed out from the terminal, up over a hill, disappeared down the other side, ending at the top of a 500 foot cliff. Departing flights vanished behind this hill before they soared up into view again once airborne. Flying inbound, I knew there should be pavement just over the lip of this cliff but for the moment all I could see was a sheer sandstone cliff. A small troop of baboons on the rocks stopped their nit picking and watched our landing gear pass overhead. Our pilot leveled out at just the right moment putting us 20 feet off the ground when our shadow topped the cliff, five seconds before touchdown.

We hauled our tote bags down a mobile ladder and across the tarmac to the terminal. Here, 5000 feet above sea level, the morning was cool and bright. Spring rains had brushed the distant hills with green. Across a gully, the rag-tag informal edge of Maseru had crept further up the hillside since I was last here. Without pavement, running water, sewers, electricity or much of anything else, this clot of humans and huts was little more than a squatter camp, filled with people eking out a living through odd jobs and petty theft in town. After getting an entry stamp on my passport, an embassy friend met me outside the terminal, dropped me at the Lesotho Hilton, and left with, "You get cleaned up. I'll be back for you later. Cocktails at 1900 hours." He sounded insistent and left me wondering why.

Diplomatic cocktail parties are an odd institution, an oxymoron in the foreign service since the cocktails practically eliminate any chance of serious diplomacy. Embassy staffers relax from their high tension jobs, hide from political uncertainties outside the compound walls, chase each other's spouses, and exchange mildly disparaging comments about "the locals" and their weird customs, all of it lubricated by tax-free alcohol from the commissary. There are, however, exceptions and tonight would be one of them.

I arrived at the party to find that almost everyone I had worked with when I lived here was still at post. Even the new Ambassador, Keith Brown, a Colorado businessman, was at the party tonight. Just after his appointment by President Reagan, my wife and I had briefed Keith in his Denver office on the special nature of Lesotho and some of its government's inner workings. This night handshakes and laughter filled the room as we veterans of years living in the Mountain Kingdom of Lesotho reunited. I felt right at home. Familiar acronyms and insider meanings sprinkled through our conversation. *This is gonna be a good trip*, I thought, anticipating productivity and fun. I poured myself two fingers of untaxed Jack Daniels over ice.

Before the conversation really got started, someone suggested that I might talk with Keith for a minute. I found him in the study down the hall. As I entered, others there with him found reasons to leave. This meeting would obviously be private, one-on-one, which seemed odd for an otherwise routine cocktail party. We chatted for a few minutes, catching up on events since our meeting in Denver and on his first reactions to being a diplomat instead of a businessman. Then he got right to his point.

"Jerry, someone wants to meet with you. Unofficially. Out of the office. We could arrange it at my house where it can be completely private. Can you come 'round to the Residence tomorrow night?"

"Sure," I answered. As an afterthought, I asked, "Who is this person, anyway?"

Keith paused, then motioned that I should follow him out into the back yard, away from the crowd and the walls and the electronics. This was as close as we could get to a Top Secret environment without the hassle of driving across town to an inner room at the embassy. Once we were outside, muffled by peach trees and Kikuyu grass, he continued,

"There are only three people who know of this meeting. You, me and your visitor and it must stay that way. Listen, this is critical. OK?"

"Absolutely." I said with emphasis. He seemed satisfied and continued.

"His Majesty, King Moshoeshoe II, has been reading your project's report and wants to discuss it with you. He said it might take an hour or more. And he is adamant that no one know he is coming. I think you know that the politicians won't let him talk to foreign missions. But, as you know, the Residence is legally American soil under international law so I suggested he meet with you there. He has to come after dark. We're set for 9:00 tomorrow night if that's OK with you. Why don't you come around at about 8:00 and we can discuss some preliminaries?"

155

Trying to lighten the moment with a bit of levity, I think I said something coy like, "I think I can fit His Majesty into my schedule. 8:00 will work just fine."

"See you tomorrow night, then." Keith turned back toward the party.

I stood there alone in the night under a peach tree, stunned with the magnitude of what just happened, a feeling which, if you are very lucky, may occur once or twice in a forty-year career. Here I was, a mere associate professor from a modest land grant university in the rather staid geographic middle of the United States. And the sovereign King of an African nation, Paramount Chief to an entire ethnic people, wanted to sit down for a couple of hours, one-on-one, and chat?

* * *

Four years earlier, in 1977, I brought a team of development economists and geographers from Colorado State University to Lesotho. Our job was to work within the Ministry of Agriculture, to train their staff in policy analysis and to do research that would support recommended changes in agricultural policy. Collectively with our Ministry counterparts, we were the Lesotho Agricultural Sector Analysis (LASA) project. Because our project was funded by the United States Agency for International Development, we were part of America's foreign policy.

Did Lesotho really matter to the outside world? As only a dot the size of Maryland on the African map, probably not much. But for a brief period it was a pawn on a grand geopolitical game board. Both the Cold War and the anti-apartheid conflict had their little sideshows in Lesotho. The Soviet Union, with sinister intent, thought that a socialist Lesotho, geographically inside South Africa, would help to destabilize the latter and weaken its ties to the west. Anti-apartheid guerillas sometimes used bases in Lesotho to launch raids on police stations and other targets across the border. The South African Defense Force would then follow them home and we could hear machine guns rattling at the border. Western donor nations flooded the place with money and attention, driven more by political than humanitarian concerns. Largely oblivious to all this, our CSU team flew off to Maseru full of a messianic commitment to do good works, extend our university's mission to the wider world stage, dispense knowledge and "save" this one little corner of Africa from hunger, poverty and misery.

The LASA project had both success, and some misses. Two and a half years into our three-year project, our educational goals were well met. The sector analysis research, however, languished, barely outlined with only bits of preliminary work completed. The Ministry of Agriculture seemed to have other ideas, assigning the CSU team to various daily administrative crises. We felt like we were always putting out brush fires. With only six months to go, the Permanent Secretary for Central Planning, who outranked our agricultural bosses, ordered the sector analysis pushed to the front burner. I started an end-of-project research and writing crush which produced the LASA document, all 302 pages of it. I wrote nearly three-quarters of it myself. Completed in 1980, I titled it, "Toward the Year 2000" to stress its 20-year forward view.

USAID embraced our document wholeheartedly. They reprinted and handed out over a thousand copies, until it lay on every desk or bookshelf in Lesotho's Ministry of Agriculture, the Central Planning and Development Office, Cabinet offices and elsewhere. In 1981, USAID wanted to redesign their agricultural programs in Lesotho around the LASA recommendations. They flew me to Maseru for three weeks of creative word-smithing, converting my report into their programs for Congressional and AID/Washington approval.

Meanwhile, unknown to the Americans, His Majesty had been reading "Toward the Year 2000." Now he wanted to talk.

I arrived at the Ambassador's Residence at exactly 8:00 p.m. I stood in his living room, too nervous to sit. The "preliminaries" Keith wanted to talk about were largely protocols, such as when to address the king as "Your Majesty," when to use "Sir," and when to use the Sesotho term *Morena*. Little things, but important in his circle. He offered a single Jack Daniels. I accepted.

The knock on the door at nine o'clock was barely audible. But Keith heard it, stopped in mid-sentence and headed toward the foyer. *Well, here goes nothin!* crept across my mind. I stood up, almost too rigidly, and waited. The two of them returned, His Majesty gliding across the room with a tangible grace. Slender, well over six feet tall, with intelligent, understanding eyes, he carried a commanding presence. Yet his demeanor was soft, unobtrusive. I relaxed ever so slightly. We were introduced. I replied with the specified "Your Majesty." We shook hands; I tried to match his soft grip. In his left hand he held a copy of "Toward the Year 2000." Along its top edge was a thicket of paper clips marking passages we would discuss. He asked about my time in Lesotho, although he probably already knew a great deal since his nephew and personal aide had done some seasonal research for our project. After a few minutes of pleasantries, Keith led us out to chairs on his veranda. He then offered and served tea himself, the servants having been sent away tonight to ensure the king's privacy. Once we got into the subject of agricultural and development policies for Lesotho, Keith left us alone in the warm night, sliding the heavy glass door shut behind himself. It was after 10:30 when we let ourselves back into his living room.

The king, although wholly dedicated to his people, was imprisoned by politics within a largely ceremonial monarchy. Still, our discussion was brisk and thorough. We focused on economic opportunities for villagers with their impoverished two- and three-acre farms and the policies and technologies that might help them prosper. We talked of crops and livestock, national food security, soil conservation, exports to South Africa, off-farm jobs, stimuli for small agribusinesses, and more. His LASA book had paper clips in every chapter. In fact, it felt a lot like my doctoral dissertation defense. The King was a man of his people. He knew Lesotho's farms and villages intimately, and his questions were penetrating. He suggested programs or policies I had not thought of.

"My country used to be an internationally important exporter of Merino wool and mohair. Our mohair was so pure that it was known as "Basotho Blue mohair" and brought the highest price. Can't you add a program to bring those days back?"

"Your report needs more emphasis on food self-sufficiency. It is so embarrassing to rely on South Africa all the time for maize. They can hold us hostage by threatening to shut off our maize supplies"

"We need more labor-intensive crops so the men can come home from the South African mines. Can't we expand our asparagus production or start table grapes for export to Europe?"

I was learning fast. It became obvious that we shared a great deal; values, ethics, our commitment to the poor. We found ourselves talking almost as friends with common cause as the evening wore on.

Somewhere in our second hour we reached the LASA recommendations that agricultural policy be redirected wholly toward small-scale farming. As happens often in Africa, the largest share of government's subsidies and technical support found its way to the farms of the Prime Minister, his Cabinet members and other political cronies. Less privileged families found themselves last in the queue. Many remained abjectly poor, even hungry, with their households torn apart by the necessity of the men migrating to work across the border in South Africa to earn a living wage.

Yet the theory I had advocated in Pakistan and would soon preach to South Africa showed that Lesotho would be better served if incomes flowed directly to the poor, leaving the rich to profit from the incomes and spending of a growing middle class. I asked why the government seemed unable to understand that principle. His eyes downcast, he said, almost under his breath, that maybe the "Honorable Ministers" had other priorities.

Unfortunately, frustration got the better of me; my voice escaped its chains.

"Why?" I demanded. "Can't they see what they are doing to this country? The people go hungry while the politicians prosper."

It was a challenge I wished I had never uttered. He started to answer but his voice caught in his throat. He fell silent. And so did I. I sat there, wanting to take back those words, wanting to change things for my new friend and his people.

I looked across at him, seeking guidance on how to proceed, or just a sign that I had not been too offensive with my outburst. He did not speak for a few long seconds. Then I saw a single tear descend his umber cheek. That's when it all came crashing home for me. The powerlessness of a figurehead monarch, the futility of his passion and commitment suffocated by self-serving politicians, the squander of foreign assistance, indeed the whole hopeless morass that was Africa in 1981, where politics and greed trumped the people's welfare and their futures all too often. My eyes were moist as well.

In many ways, Lesotho is a microcosm of Africa. The nation gained independence in 1966 after 98 years as a British protectorate. The departing Brits recognized Moshoeshoe II as Paramount Chief, or King. And yet they installed Leabua Jonathon, head of the opposing political party, as Prime Minister. With its tribal culture, its leadership split and polarized, Lesotho wasn't ready for a constitutional monarchy and an electoral democracy.

A tragicomedy ensued as African political theater ran amuck. In 1970, the nation's first popular elections brought overwhelming victory to the King's party. Despite receiving only 35 percent of the vote Jonathon's party, in power at the time, decided that while elections had been "interesting," there was no real need to relinquish power. So they suspended the constitution, imprisoned the newly elected government, and began to rule by decree and military force. It took 16 years before this Western oddity of popular elections was tried again. During those years, a military junta overthrew Jonathon's government. Then a second junta overthrew the first. This second general stripped the king of power and sent him to Oxford University "for further studies." The military then placed the King's son, Letsie, on the throne, assuming he would behave as instructed. However, acting now with the powers of King, Letsie dismissed the generals, overthrew the government they had set up, and then abdicated in favor of his father who cut his "studies" short to resume the throne.

It would have been hilarious if the human costs had not been so high. Assassinations occurred on both sides. Court proceedings were shams. South Africa tried to intervene and gave up. A consortium of southern African nations sent peace-keeping troops. Foreign assistance missions pulled out when staff members got caught in the crossfire. The police joined sides with various politicians, leaving civil law and order to an African mafia, which took *de facto* control of the national capital. Innocents died. Development regressed. And a rampant civil service brain drain stripped government of its best professionals as they sought employment abroad. Even working in South Africa under the hated apartheid system was better than this. Safer too.

In tribal Africa they say, "A chief is a chief *by* the people," meaning that only by the will of the people does an individual earn the respect and thus the authority of a true chief.

Moshoeshoe II was highly regarded, even revered. His namesake, King Moshoeshoe I, had founded Lesotho in the 1830s, gathering the allegiance of scattered settlements, centralizing some authority, developing a network of regional and village chiefs and a rudimentary set of national laws. In name, influence, status and wisdom, Moshoeshoe II bore his royal lineage well.

To Jonathon, however, the king's power and influence were threats. For twenty years, he and his party henchmen worked to strip the chieftainship of its roles in governance and social leadership. Little by little they succeeded, until only a ceremonial monarchy remained.

* * *

While in Maseru, we lived across the street from a unique man, Victor Ntsekhe, his wife Julia, and their son, Mpiko. The Eckerts and the Ntsekhes were drawn together by the antics of our boys who were fast friends. Victor had completed his college pre-med studies across the border in South Africa at the University of the Witwatersrand. Even in the heyday of apartheid, he was elected president of the student body, the first black man ever to hold that distinction. Victor went on to complete his medical studies in England, specializing in psychiatry. When he returned, I believe he was the first fully credentialed black African psychiatrist on the continent. Victor built the government's mental health hospital in Maseru and served as its director and chief psychiatrist for the rest of his life.

He also maintained a private practice to augment his modest government salary from the mental hospital.

Juxtaposed among his private patients were two very important clients: Prime Minister Leabua Jonathon and His Majesty Moshoeshoe II. His two principal clients and their warring political parties battled each other for years over control of their nation. Victor died an early death, in part from hypertension. After his death, I learned a couple of things that kept him from sleeping well at night. One was the challenge of convincing the Prime Minister to let the king live, and to grant him at least ceremonial roles. The other was convincing His Majesty to accept those ceremonial roles so that the Basotho people through their network of chiefs would have at least some place in government. The alternative could have been civil war.

I am quite certain that Victor Ntsekhe almost single-handedly kept the lid on that volatile pot for years. I also know that it cost him his health, and in the end, his life. When Victor died, I was one of only four or five white faces among the 5000 mourners at his funeral. What we all saw there will never be forgotten. In a show of profound and humble respect, His Majesty, King Moshoeshoe II donned the sheepskins of a peasant, walked overnight for miles from his palace to the cemetery, and stood there silently in salute as Victor's coffin was lowered. Through him, the nation of Lesotho honored Dr. Victor Ntsekhe.

* * *

Leabua Jonathon, Victor Ntsekhe, and His Majesty, Moshoeshoe II are all gone now, leaving me as the only living witness to this bit of Africana. Yes, it may be just a small story of two men sharing an intense moment on a veranda, but it is also a larger story of the African abyss. In His Majesty's eyes I saw that Africa weep, its soul recently martyred to greed and grasping power. I saw an Africa that brought its royal best to tears. Until that moment, it never occurred to me that kings might cry. Just a few short years later, his niece, Manapo Moshoeshoe, my protégé and colleague on the LASA project, and my dear friend, was murdered because, in trying to serve her people, she got too close to local politics. My Africa died there with her in front of a machine gun on a mountain road. Just a few years after that, His Majesty died in a car wreck, one that may not have been so accidental after all, assassinated by those same dark forces. Or so the voices whisper. We can never know for sure. The mechanic rumored to have found the severed brake lines disappeared.

Today, His Majesty's country languishes, still a developmental challenge that never reached its potential. My three years working for his people, the hardest years in my career, have apparently gone for naught. Every now and then, on a warm summer moonlit night, in the shadows of my own back porch, I think I see him weeping still.

"Never doubt that a small group of thoughtful people can change the world. Indeed, it's the only thing that ever has."

~Margaret Meade

Swakop Beginnings

Swakopmund, a quiet little town with an exotic name meaning the mouth of the Swakop River, lies on the west coast of Namibia. A German name in Africa, a town I never heard of, in a country I had never visited. Intriguing.

After WWI, the League of Nations stripped Germany it of its colonies and gave German Southwest Africa to South Africa as a trust territory. Seventy-three years later South Africa reluctantly cut this chunk of mostly desert loose and Namibia was born in March 1990.

Four months later, the International Association of Agricultural Economists organized a regional conference there, partly to welcome this new country into the broader agricultural development community. Sub-rosa, South Africa footed most of the bill and the Agricultural Economics Association of South Africa provided the leg work. Small subterfuges like this kept South Africa's academics in modest contact with the rest of the world despite the academic boycott then in place. The conference would meet in Swakopmund, known simply as Swakop to the locals. I scrounged some university funding and packed my bags.

167

The conference theme, "Restructuring Southern Africa's Agriculture," recognized a region in significant flux, in its agriculture as well as in most every other way. Namibia was now free with a popularly elected black government for the first time in its history. Uncertain waters lay ahead. South Africa, itself, inched its way toward democracy – finally. The autocrat, Hastings Banda, Malawi's President for Life for the previous 29 years, was losing his iron grip. His country wobbled. Under Robert Mugabe, Zimbabwe launched a disastrous land reform, expropriating productive white-owned farms and giving them to "freedom fighters," driving the country's farm sector into the ground and turning a thriving exporter of farm crops into an international beggar of food aid. A circus of coups, counter coups, assassinations and power struggles embroiled Lesotho. War weary and broke, Cuba stood on the brink of pulling their military out, leaving a power vacuum in Angola and Mozambique. And the Russians were finding that they could no longer afford to support the "armed struggles" of various liberation movements across the region.

After years drafting agricultural policies for Lesotho, I believed I had something to offer for the wider region. Barry Hill, a former USAID agricultural officer in Lesotho, and I wrote a paper with the fancy title, "Agricultural Development Priorities for Namibia: The Lessons from Lesotho." Presumptuous, perhaps, for two guys who had never been to Namibia, but a bit of presumption flavors much of the foreign assistance game.

I don't know if anyone ever read our paper after the conference. The Berlin Wall fell in 1989 and the Soviet Union collapsed in 1991. US foreign assistance swung almost immediately to rehabilitating and de-communizing the former East Bloc. Our foreign policy, writ large, seemed to be that democracy and capitalism were the best of all worlds for everyone, especially the people who had lived under socialist dictatorships. Namibia was largely forgotten in Washington, as were many other African nations of no strategic value. I suppose it doesn't matter now whether our paper had an impact or not. Something else happened in Swakop during the conference that probably affected millions.

* * *

Several threads from the warp and weft of my life came together about then. For one, in Pakistan I had seen deep, pervasive poverty and winced at the misery it brought to daily life. I crafted what I thought were novel solutions but an all too familiar, entrenched system of greed and corruption got in the way. South Africa suffered the same degrading poverty but the cleavage between rich and poor fell along racial lines, enforced by the hated laws of apartheid. The worst statistical measure of inequality ever calculated at national level was South Africa's. Given its racial dimension, here was a powder keg just waiting for a fuse. Again, I offered solutions. This time at least some people listened.

Fairness and distributive justice had become my new passion, one which spilled over into the classroom. My graduate course on income inequality and economic growth used John Rawls' *Theory of Justice* as a central text. Arguably the leading moral philosopher of the 20th Century, Rawls defined a negotiating process to achieve "perfect fairness" which, he wrote, would then lead to a perfect framework for human rights. In South Africa, democracy and a new Constitution lay on the horizon and with them, a new Bill of Rights. They were about to rewrite their rules for fairness. Rumor had it that Nelson Mandela along with Walter Sisulu and Govan Mbeki had spent their time while breaking rocks on their Robben Island prison debating the structure for a perfect nation. With centuries of colonialism, racism and apartheid as their point of departure, I expected a path breaking statement of human rights to emerge someday soon. And I wanted to help.

My new passion also led me to the International Development Ethics Association (IDEA). I joined and attended the IDEA conference at Merida, Mexico in 1989. South Africa was much discussed there, by social scientists, clergy and by committed practitioners who worked for justice at the village level. I came away wondering, if the rest of the world could talk openly about an ethic for South Africa, why had I never heard it discussed in the halls of power in Pretoria? I worked with, drank coffee with, and partied with people who served in South Africa's government at its highest professional levels. And I never heard anybody talking of ethics. In discussions with the ethicists at Merida, I finally saw this as a serious anomaly. Why shouldn't ethics be openly discussed and used to underpin social policy?

* * *

During the decades that German South-West Africa existed as a colony, Swakopmund served as its sea port despite the lack of a deep water dock. To handle cargo ships, the colony built a jetty, some 50 feet wide extending over

170

1000 feet out into the waves. No longer in commercial use, the jetty serves today as a nostalgic reminder of Namibia's early history, a tourist attraction, a site for pier fishermen, and a venue for social functions.

On this jetty, the Mayor of Swakopmund, resplendent with mayoral sash and medallions across his chest, his voluble personality on full display, hosted a cocktail party for conferees the night we arrived. There, enjoying Windhoek Lager and grilled sausages in a brisk ocean breeze, I found several friends from Pretoria, colleagues with whom I had worked over the years on income inequality and development policy for South Africa and the region. With all of us reunited again, this would be an enjoyable conference, maybe even productive.

I found Nick Vink and Johan van Rooyan leaning over the railing watching waves splash against the pilings. Nearer to shore small, foamy crests rode the breakers in, lit by a rising moon. These two had been the catalysts who made this conference a reality. I wandered over, stein of beer in hand, and leaned out over the water with them.

"Professor Eckert," Johan said in greeting, with a slap on the back and a bone crushing handshake. Johan had his own doctorate in agricultural economics but he liked to kid me about my exalted title.

"Glad you could make it. We were afraid you might be tied up with classes back home," added Nick.

"Hey, I wouldn't have missed this for the world," I said. "I assigned the students a two-week long research paper, which, of course they will compete in the last 48 hours before it's due. They're probably enjoying their holiday from class, but not as much as I am"

171

We chatted a bit, catching up on who was here, who was not, how the South African government had secretly funded the conference, and other minutia. I asked them if anyone ever explicitly brought ethics into current policy debates. Neither could recall any such discussion. For blacks, the basic decisions about their human rights had been entrenched in law years ago by the framers of apartheid. Who they could marry, where they could live, what jobs they could seek, if they could vote or hold office; an iron grid of social control proscribed these and many other basic rights. If change was in the wind, those discussions were kept out of sight.

Of course moral content underlay many debates. But to openly discuss fairness and human rights, apparently wasn't done at the policy level. In the press and other media, discussion of the moral ground, lay mostly buried under angry accusations, assertions of each others' inhumanity, and threats of violence. Two monologues passing each other by in the heat of differing sets of fears and hatreds.

I didn't know it that night, but that seminal word "ethics" took root and sprouted. The next day, "ethics" or "rights" dropped unobtrusively into two or three of the papers given by others, often hanging on the end like an afterthought, or brought up in the Q & A sessions. Participants seemed interested. Their offhand remarks had substance. Obviously they had been thinking through pieces of the puzzle, each in their own way.

Bingo! An idea. A voice in my head asked, "Why not?" And then "Why not now?"

At the lunch break, I went looking for Nick again. He directed the Center for Policy Analysis at the Development Bank for Southern Africa and was my boss when I worked there. The Bank and Nick had pulled this conference together and he knew everybody in the Pretoria contingent.

"Nick. We've got 90 minutes between the last speech of the day and the cocktail hour. Let's get some of our guys together, find a room, and talk about ethics for the New South Africa."

Nick picked up on my excitement, saw the potential, and quickly became a co-conspirator. We decided it should be a small group of people we trusted to make a contribution. We divided up names and moved through the conference attendees during a coffee break.

"Some of us are getting together later to sketch out what might be included in an 'Ethics Charter' for the New South Africa. I'd like you to join us."

Everyone we asked accepted. I located a room with a long whiteboard at one end. Just because it seemed right at the time, I also organized a round of beer; Windhoek Lager, Namibia's best. Around 3:30, nine friends filtered into the room, closed the door and we got started. Around me sat one other American, one Swede and six South Africans, only one of whom was black. Nearly all had doctorates in agricultural economics. The two other foreigners came from universities, the South Africans all from the Development Bank. The guys shifted their chairs around until a loose semi-circle emerged, opening toward the white board where I stood, marker in hand. I started the meeting by observing that an ethics dialogue seemed strangely absent for a country about to completely redefine itself. Especially given the enormity of the changes ahead. That touched a chord. The conversation exploded as everyone jumped in. Ideas, questions, analyses of past causes, suggested future policies, flooded through the room. I struggled to capture it all on the board while throwing in the occasional question to steer things along.

Rarely does a clutch of colleagues share a common cause with such passion. Yet, what could a bunch of mostly white guys, technicians and analysts, offer to a nation soon be ruled by its overwhelming black majority with vastly different politics? We had no guarantee of success, but we felt we had to try. We felt a need to open up this wholly new arena of ethics in the debate about South Africa's future. Our final paper, a manifesto of sorts, began with:

An element missing in the South African dialogue today is an explicit consideration of ethics. . . . Current debate revolves around technical details, preconditions for negotiations, alternative constitutional options . . . Yet the fundamental problem in South Africa is ethical, not procedural. The contest is being fought over the route to the future without first choosing the destination. The nation's collective ethic, the 'basic moral character,' of the population has yet to be clearly articulated.

South Africa's vast diversity almost demanded agreement on a common moral identity. We listed two justifications. First, we wanted to convince all sides that discussing ethics, searching for that 'basic moral character," should not frighten anyone. In fact, we felt sure that only with an agreed ethic could a peaceful nonracial future be reached. It was the alternative that we found frightening. The struggle between two races, so polarized by apartheid, could only lead to bloodshed if it continued without a new, shared morality. We wrote:

People of all colors are being asked to re-examine their most fundamental beliefs about each other. . . . Both black and white find themselves searching their souls on this issue. . . . Those who (succeed) have had to reach down within themselves to find a deep rooted humanism, an ethic that often differs greatly from their early socialization and life experience. (Even so,) individual answers are not sufficient. What is needed is a communally forged ethic . . . which becomes a framework of values, laws and practices. An open dialogue could accelerate and focus this needed transition.

Our next justification appealed to people on both sides of the color line to discover their common membership in the human race.

Second, if all contesting parties could put their basic ethics explicitly on the table, how different would they be? Might not all South Africans, white and black, find that they share a common humanism? In the bedrock of an ethical dialogue could lay shared values concerning human worth that can support an egalitarian, nonviolent future.

For those of us from the western nations, these assertions seem automatic, the "givens" of a structure of human rights. Yet the fact that these explicit words were needed, out on the table for open discussion in South Africa in 1990 was a measure of the state of antagonisms, fears, even hatreds existing at the time. We felt the time was right, that an opening existed to ground the future explicitly on an ethics foundation, so we put it all out there in print. As the group discussed this last point, our central long-term objective became clear:

The most significant impact of agreement on ethical principles could be the initial structure of a Bill of Rights.

At that time, South Africa bristled when the rest of the world prescribed or proscribed to them. Laws, rules, constitutional forms, and basic behavioral modes – it seemed that everyone outside the country wanted to enforce their "outsider" views of what ought to happen. And not without reason. Apartheid in all its sinister manifestations blighted the human conscience. South Africa, however, seemed unable to change, not because they didn't know by now that apartheid was wrong, that it was doomed, but more likely because their pride would not let them knuckle under to dictates from abroad. It's also possible that they didn't have the answers, that the way forward was unknown to policy makers blinded by their entrenched past. It also may have been just a little frightening. Sentiment among whites tended more along the lines of "Leave us alone. It's our problem. We'll fix it." The group in Swakop tackled this by affirming the country's right to direct its own future. Yet we also kept those outside pressures on the table as a reminder of the need for urgent action. In short, if the country could be seen heading toward an acceptable end result, then the rest of the world should leave them alone to find their way. We needed to assure white South Africa that we were on their side as well. Otherwise, they would never accept our proposed ethics.

One case that South Africa has not made well is that in the final analysis, the right to self determination must be respected. Perhaps the missing bit of persuasive logic is also ethical. . . . certain norms regarding human rights have international support. Compliance is expected from any country seeking acceptance in the community of modern nations. (For South Africa) a commitment to a moral end result should earn the right to define the process and the desired final product through the nation's own internal processes.

176

One of the theories of distributive justice separates the goals of equality and equity. Equality applies to life's social and political domains while equity, or rewards according to some standard, applies to the economic domain.

Simply stated, the equality principle in social and political domains asserts that every human being is of equal worth as a result of their humanity alone and that the fabric of society and its political system must be woven to fit each person in equal measure.

Without saying so, this statement targeted the white population, which was trying to unlearn deeply embedded moral "truths," a matrix of beliefs built upon the presumed inferiority of Blacks, which allowed for their suppression and dehumanization. Truths, as one of them said to me for emphasis, that they had learned on their grandmother's knee. Then we hit apartheid squarely in the gut with the moral theory of John Rawls.

Rawls, in his fundamental work, Theory of Justice, translates this ethic (of equality) specifically into equal rights to freedom of thought and speech, freedom of conscience (religion and cultural affinity) freedom of assembly, freedom from arbitrary arrest and seizure, freedom to hold office, the right to vote, freedom of movement and choice of occupation and residence.

Apartheid's rules, regulations and habitual behaviors essentially denied or abridged every single one of these for black and mixed race populations. We were saying this had to change. No equivocation. Of course, the outside world was demanding these things as well, but those of us in Swakopmund sensed that our "internal" document might carry more weight in the longer run.

These . . . constitute widely held beliefs in the modern world. They also form the ethical standards which apartheid is accused of violating.

I then steered our discussion to the third domain of life, to economics, the one with the different ethic. Most of the Swakop group had graduated in agricultural economics or development economics and we had much to say. Among apartheid's laws were the hated Job Reservation Acts. Legally only whites could hold most positions of responsibility, skilled positions with higher salaries. Blacks were relegated largely to unskilled labor. These rules had to go. It would be so easy, we thought. A single stroke of a pen could fix things.

In the economic domain, the basic expectation is the right of equal opportunity. All persons should have the opportunity to advance themselves to the full limits of their capabilities. . . . The labor market must differentiate between workers only on the basis of merit and performance.

But as we drafted that thought, we began to see "equal opportunity" as a cruel joke, given the legacies of apartheid. We went further with a carefully worded conclusion.

The goal of equal opportunity raises a derivative concern in South Africa. Enormous differentials in capability exist today as a result of apartheid, its precursor of social discrimination, widespread poverty and other social limitations. Simply ensuring an equal chance at the future is not enough when the capabilities of many have been artificially lowered by past practices. In South Africa, one must supplement equal opportunity with the right to an equal start. Not only does everyone run life's race on the same track, they must each begin from the same starting line.

With this, the group hoped to place the idea of affirmative action, tailored to local conditions, squarely in the middle of South Africa's agenda.

This cannot be achieved easily or quickly. It implies massive redistribution of education, training and opportunities toward those previously excluded from the mainstream. Accepting this goal redirects government toward comprehensive affirmative action investments. The challenge reaches far beyond removing apartheid's restrictions to include erasing its legacies of inequality and constrained capabilities.

To gain the support of white owned businesses, which must bear the brunt of the costs of retraining their labor, our logic emphasized efficiency gains that should flow directly from greater labor mobility and access to skills training. We stressed that the ethic of proportional rewards set a clear incentive for honest individual effort. As the labor force (mostly black) responded to these incentives, efficiencies would rise as would business profits (largely white owned) as well as the economic surplus (which government could capture with taxes) and reinvest in additional ways to remove apartheid's legacies. We were painting a win-win picture, one in which we firmly believed. We wanted to allay the fears many had of zero-sum redistributions where the gains of the poor came directly from losses by the rich. In this we mirrored the World Bank's three decade long policy of "redistribution from growth." It also just might be politically feasible.

To economists, proportional rewards mean the more the work or the output from work, the higher the pay. This is considered "fair," or ethically just in the non-Communist

179

world. However, we all knew that society also needs a safety net. We included this thought.

Beliefs about distributive justice include one important modification to the ethic of rewards in proportion to productivity. For whatever reason, there will be large numbers of people whose maximum efforts fail to meet their most basic needs of food, shelter, clothing and a minimum of social experience. Intervention to ensure basic needs for all people is considered a just mandate for modern nations and a just expectation on the part of their constituencies.

The safety net concept sets a floor below which proportional reward should not fall. We also suggested, rather tongue in cheek, a ceiling on incomes at the upper end of the spectrum. Our justification was that political instability often results from huge income gaps, a lesson I had learned in Pakistan.

Certainly large gaps lead to economic segregation with large portions of society remaining outside the mainstream. These gaps undermine both equal opportunity in the economic sphere and equal political liberty. Existing inequalities in South Africa are sufficiently paralyzing to require that the question at least be considered.

But when I wrote this, income inequality in South Africa was the worst ever measured. I doubted that anyone in power would take seriously the suggestion that an upper limit should cap personal incomes. But economic inequality festered as a key source of violent unrest and needed attention.

Our treatment of political rights put forth many of the basics that most of us in the West take for granted although we may not practice them fully. South Africa, however, remained in the political dark ages. Their black population,

180

more than 75 percent of the country, had never voted. Decennial censuses didn't even count blacks until 1980. And their main political party, the African National Congress, had been, until recently banned from the country and from participating in politics.

We affirm two fundamental ethical principles for the political sphere. First, the people have a right to be heard. Government . . . must recognize the moral mandates of their constituencies. Second, the right to political activity and the right to vote are globally accepted principles.

We thought it important to add another right drawn specifically from African political realities. Press reports of threat and counter-threat had raised this as an issue in many minds.

Recent discussions in South Africa suggest another important right, that being security of expectations, or freedom from ugly political surprises. Suddenly suspended constitutions, states of emergency under which rights are suspended, and other rude shocks which erase carefully crafted ethical structures have occurred too frequently in recent African history.

Looking to the future from Swakopmund in 1990, we could see that South Africa stood on the brink of an unprecedented transformation. Mandela would soon be released from prison. His political party would be allowed to function freely. Releasing the energies of 75 percent of the population, those shackled with apartheid's hundreds of laws and regulations, would change everything. Global history offered no analogs from which to learn. An unimaginable future lay ahead. Yet one dynamic could be clearly predicted. To get from 1990 to what folks called the "New South Africa," much would be reallocated. Putting redistribution out on the table would get people thinking and just might soften the blow.

Redistributions will come in all domains; in power, in property, in incomes and wealth and in social and political opportunity. It seems likely that this process . . . will most clearly galvanize people into formulating their underlying values. Two ethical issues will arise; just how much redistribution is 'fair' and what criteria will govern the process? Without answers to these questions, the fear of unrestrained and arbitrary expropriation may paralyze and inflame the reform process.

The Swakop Group recommended embedding redistribution in a constitution, based on a fully enfranchised political consensus and backed up by the courts. This, we thought, would add stability to the process since constitutions aren't often amended. Then we tried shifting the dialogue from redistributing property and wealth, an inflammatory zero-sum game, to redistributing access and opportunity, a process whereby gains by the winners do not necessarily come at the expense of others. Redistributing access rests on institutional change, often an easier, less explosive, road than others.

Our penultimate point focused on forgiveness. As one means of healing, the country would one day establish a Truth and Reconciliation Commission headed by Nobel Laureate Archbishop Desmond Tutu. This process insisted on an open admission of guilt, and a display of heartfelt remorse before true forgiveness was possible. Our statement in Swakop anticipated this.

It would be grossly unrealistic to expect the past to be forgotten. Today's cultures and attitudes are very much a product of recent experience. One could, however, hope for a measure of forgiveness under certain conditions. These are that each side openly accepts responsibility for their past actions, sets out to correct undesirable results and commits to a future molded around humane ethics. Of these the dominant expectation is an open admission of culpability without which the prospects of forgiveness are slim.

Finally, in 1990 the white government was unwinding apartheid by removing one law or rule after another in a slow creep toward dissolving the system. While they trumpeted those steps to the world to show their progress, we didn't think it was nearly fast nor decisive enough.

South Africa must move from the relatively passive stance of removing or suspending the laws of segregation to the proactive position of outlawing discrimination and then enforcing that stance. . . . There is a great difference between 'the government shall not discriminate' and 'the government finds discrimination illegal.'

Ninety minutes of intense exchange with everyone at full alert had left us drained. We had given the topic everything we had. Our best thoughts hung there, stippled with multicolored dry-erase markers across a white board extending the full width of a large meeting room. Bringing the meeting to a close, I sent everyone off to the cocktail hour and sat down to record every word, asterisk and underlining on the wall. Johan van Rooyan slipped back in with a liter stein of cold, very welcome Windhoek Lager Draught.

"I thought you might need one of these," he said. "That was a really great discussion. Nice job." He looked at the hieroglyphics on the board for a minute and then went back to the party outside.

It was another one of those ethereal moments when you sense that something precious just happened. Again, I can only describe it as a feeling of detachment, my body floating. I looked at that wall and I thought I could see the future of a nation, still poor, still struggling, but just maybe with a greater measure of peace and dignity for all its peoples. I couldn't speak.

* * *

The conference ended next day and I flew home. During part of the transatlantic crossing I organized and expanded my notes copied from the white board, wanting to capture every nuance while they were still fresh. What happened next still amazes me.

I arrived home on Sunday night. By Tuesday afternoon I had finished the penultimate draft of "Toward an Ethic for a New South Africa." By Thursday evening, it had been reviewed by professors of philosophy and political science at Colorado State University, a visiting justice on the South African Supreme Court and a senior editor at National Geographic. On Friday it went by e-mail to each member of the Swakop Group urgently requesting comments and refinements. By Monday they had all responded suggesting minimal edits. Tuesday morning, only ten days after the conference, the final paper crossed the Atlantic again attached to an e-mail to Nick Vink. Within hours Nick had it in the hands of Simon Brand, Director General of the Development Bank, former Economic Advisor to the Prime Minister and intellectual pillar of the Afrikaner establishment.

Within days, ethical principles began to appear in the internal discussions of government.

I can't measure the impact, if any, of the Swakop Group's work that week. Certainly no government agency had asked for this effort. We probably put no specific provisions into future law or the Bill of Rights when it finally emerged. After all, across the region many individuals were groping their way toward finding their inner beliefs at that point in history and hundreds if not thousands made their voices heard. What the Swakop Group did, however, was make it acceptable in policy circles, even expected, to openly discuss ethics, values and human rights. And we laid out a framework for such discussions.

In those days of the struggle, the African National Congress had their "Point of the Spear" (*Umkhonto we Sizwe*, in Xhosa), their armed wing aligned against the government in the battle for change. The Development Bank, more peacefully, served as an accessible think tank for the white government, the cutting edge of the policy debate within government. Recently Nick told me that the Swakop paper "suffused most of what came out of the Development Bank for quite a while." Our paper helped to defuse the impending battle over land reform, probably the most explosive topic on the table. And when I, with inputs from Nick and another Development Bank colleague, finally wrote an internationally acceptable economic strategy for the incoming Mandela government, it rested firmly on ethical principles, the foundation stones of which had been hewed in Swakopmund.

The Englishman

In Africa, the dead are not necessarily the dearly departed. Some remain, nearby. They can be mischievous, helpful, or downright vicious. Much depends on how we, the living, treat them.

In West Africa, the signs are hard to miss. Important spirits often live in trees. Not hiding up there in the branches, but residing in the essence of the tree itself. A place of life, of strength, of shelter. At the base of "inhabited" trees or hanging from their branches are offerings brought by villagers and supplicants; gifts of food and drink, traditional palm wine, trinkets and talismans, all for the welfare, happiness and succor of the spirit residing within. These trees, usually old and gnarled, offer tantalizing glimpses into another belief system.

I am torn. I want to believe that the evidence supports the existence of Sasquatch or that Nessie hides in the murk of a Scottish loch. I want to believe in a convergence of spiritual and secular worlds where spirits of the deceased remain an active part of family and village life. Yet without evidence, the scientist in me suggests this can't be so.

This conflict between spirits and science surfaced on one of my frequent trips to Gambia, West Africa. I served as on-campus project director for the AID funded Gambian Mixed Farming Project. We had a field team of nine scientists, living near the capital of Banjul and working with farmers and researchers throughout the country. As project director, I visited two or three times a year to assist. On one of my early trips, I noticed a massive, well-festooned, spirit tree along the highway.

That night I stayed with John Haydu, my field team agricultural economist. John was an outgoing, rambunctious, bigger-than-life character. With his size, strength and confidence, he could have been a Nebraska farm boy or football player so he called himself "thick neck" just for fun. After work, we occasionally fished for barracuda off the coast or barbecued cane rats caught by his gardener. John won the job over others because, after three years in Sierra Leone with the Peace Corps, he spoke one of Gambia's local languages and was totally at ease with the villagers up-country.

Relaxing with a beer before dinner and knowing he was a seasoned African hand, I asked what he had seen in Gambia which might have intrigued him. John was grilling a cane rat, about the size of an eight pound rabbit, turning it every few minutes. He explained how the people up-country caught them by surrounding a harvested field, clubs in hand, and then set fire to the field, chasing out the rats, snakes and anything else that might be edible.

"Hey, Big John," I asked. "What's your take on these 'spirit trees'? That one we passed on the way in from the airport – did you see all the weird stuff hanging from it?"

"They're a big part of native life here." he offered. "People believe in those spirits. They treat them with great respect, even fear. They're convinced bad things will happen if they offend the ghosts. Even our Gambian research colleagues with their foreign college degrees; they won't say they believe, but you can see they're very careful around those trees."

"What about Sierra Leone? Did you have any in your village there?"

"Yeah. The spirit of old Mama Ceesay was supposed to live in a giant kapok tree near my hut. She was an old lady witch doctor who could see the future, and had powerful juju. I never did see her but everyone said her juju protected them."

He took another swig of his beer. "While we are on this subject, I should tell you about a trip I took up-country to Sapu. Promise you won't think I've lost it?"

British colonialists had founded an agricultural research station near the village of Sapu in 1900. Our project used it as a field base. When working in that region, we all slept in the Sapu rest house, an ancient thick-walled colonial structure that stayed cool inside even in the tropical summer.

"One night I was asleep in that Sapu rest house," John began, "when something woke me. I sat up in bed, and it was like I could see right through the bedroom wall to the outside. Off in the distance something moved, it looked like an old man shuffling along. Hey, Man, believe me. I'm sitting up in bed, inside the rest house, and I'm seeing things happen outside, through the wall. Very weird. Anyway, this old man walked straight toward me. When he got closer, I could make him out, clearly a white man, but really old. His face seemed weathered, from too many years in the bush I guess. He wore a ragged shirt and shorts, some kind of colonial uniform I think."

"When he got right outside my room, he leapt up on top of the wall. Like there was no roof on that room. He sat up

189

there for a second, then he dropped down inside my bedroom. And he just stood there looking. Shit, man. Just me and this apparition, staring at each other. It could have been minutes, more likely it was only seconds, until he turned around, jumped up on top of the wall again, dropped off the other side and walked off into the bush. I don't know what he wanted, but I guess he was satisfied. Funny thing. I wasn't scared. But it was pretty amazing."

The next morning John sought out some of the local research station staff and told them about his midnight vision. They were not surprised.

"Oh yes," they said. "That's the Englishman. His ghost lives in the tree just outside the research station compound."

Since John had never heard of the Englishman, he could not have pulled this vision out of some buried memory. John did a little more digging and turned up these facts: a Brit had arrived early in the colonial era to establish the research station at Sapu. This gentleman served many years alone at Sapu, which in those days was a remote outpost. Contact with his fellow colonial officers in Banjul would have required two days travel by boat down the Gambia River. As a result, it could have been lonely duty, unless he befriended the local inhabitants, made them his family and became part of their lives. Maybe he did. Perhaps that's why his ghost never left.

I also checked. History records that this first expat scientist died there at his post, although the exact location of his grave is unknown. The local staff, those who never had their village wisdom educated out of them, took John to visit the "Englishman's tree." There he found on the ground saucers of food and drink, with amulets containing prayers hanging from the limbs.

Is there really an Englishman's ghost, a former colonial research officer, embodied in a great and ancient tree at the edge of the Sapu compound? I have no scientific proof, one way or the other. But on the banks of the Gambia River lives a village community, into which an Englishman may once have been accepted as family, and who believe his spirit is still with them. That he remains part of their community is shown by the foods they leave at the base of "his" tree. Does this spirit influence secular events? The villagers must think so because they leave their hopes and prayers on scraps of paper bound in goat skin sachets pinned to the tree. Maybe the Englishman lives only because the villagers believe that he does. Yet, they order their lives, in part, as though he were there, in the tree, watching over them. If it is all just imagination, how can I explain John's surreal experience? He identified, if only approximately, what he saw by age, sex, race and likely nationality even though he had known nothing about the Englishman beforehand.

Some months later, I found myself overnighting at Sapu on a field trip. While I didn't see the Englishman myself, I did visit his tree guided by a local staff member. I left there, on a small saucer at the base of the tree, a slice of mango, and asked, "Look after my guys on this project, would you, old man?"

191

Namib Roots

Silently a jackal circled just beyond the firelight. Twice it passed upwind. Twice its faint scent, sweet-acrid musk of cinnamon and carrion, drifted across our group. Sitting on the sand across the circle from me, the old man, my friend and our host tonight, noticed it too. I saw his chest swell, inhaling deeply to grasp the scent. His eyes turned toward the breeze, staring into darkness. Neither of us spoke of it. But on the edge of our awareness, we each added a black-backed jackal to what we knew of the surrounding night.

And this night – this night was pristine as only a night in the Namib Desert can be. A cloudless sky leaked away daytime's heat. Dry grasses moved in the breeze, touching each other's sere skins with a whisper. Quiet rustlings, the measured breath of a desert sleeping lightly. Day creatures crept away to secret hiding places while prowlers of the night emerged. The breeze took on an edge, cooling as the dark intensified.

Inside our little circle, all was warmth. As sunset faded, someone built a fire under a towering tree in this thornbush savannah. Now, we clustered there, settling to places on the sand, our skins lit orange, drinking in a radiated heat. Flames pushed back the evening chill. I leaned back, shoulders on the sand, knees blocking the campfire's blaze, my eyes adjusting to the vastness overhead. Like diamonds in black ink, a million pinpoints clustered in the southern Milky Way. Their faint light passed through the thornbush, leaving hints of shadow on the cooling sand.

My friends were all white Namibians, descendants of German colonists. Their forebears wrestled with this harsh environment to settle here and to build homes and lives from desert scrub. Each now owned a ranch passed down through generations on which they reared cattle and nurtured wildlife for hunters from abroad. We had known each other for several years, hunted together, and worked together in different ways. When work was done, we sometimes sought the solace of the desert for evenings such as this.

Politics threatened their rights to this land now and this had brought us together again. In post-colonial Africa, land reform often became an interracial flashpoint. New black electorates railed at those whites whose ownership of farms and ranches was seen as a hated vestige of historic oppression. In 1995, the feverish heat of the land debate reached Namibia, vigorously engaged by landless blacks and white farm and ranch owners. But, as one of Africa's last nations to gain independence, Namibia could learn from the checkered, sometimes ugly, history of other land reforms. Wisely, President Sam Nujoma's government threw open the debate and asked all sides, all tribes and races, for input.

We had met in the capital city, Windhoek, to draft land policy recommendations that their Agricultural Economics Association of Namibia could put on the table. The men brought their fervent hopes to the table. They spoke as trained agricultural economists yet also as ranchers deeply wanting to preserve and enhance their land, earn a living for their families and provide employment and a decent

194

livelihood for their many black workers. They invited me to their meeting because of my prior work on land reform in Pakistan, Lesotho and South Africa.

Two days of soul-searching debate left us emotionally drained. We had hammered out proposals that we hoped might be accepted within the uncertain post-colonial political milieu, but it was exhausting. We needed respite, some time with less tension, less politics. We headed for the desert, away from it all. Their wives joined us for the evening and to share a meal.

Now blue-orange flames flickered as a bed of camel thorn coals grew slowly beneath the burning brands. The fire sang with hisses, pops and laughing sounds drawn from times past, when bark lay down its woody layers, capturing moisture in its resins. Within this circle, five families renewed their friendships, caught up on each other's lives since they were last together, and welcomed me into their circle for the evening. This campfire worked as a magnet, drawing us all here from distant places. Once together, the fire seemed to soften us, moving each one gently toward inner reflections. Why, I wondered, do so many people, often from disparate cultures, respond alike to a campfire?

The men gathered here dressed in the khakis and leather of folks at home in the desert. The women did as well, with beads and bracelets as subtle flourishes. Quiet happy chatter tied the group together. They lay under a spreading camel thorn tree, the kind with canopy so high that only giraffes can browse, yet broad enough to shelter all of them. That leafy umbrella, its underside a muted glow of reflected light, caught some of the heat and sent it back toward those sprawled at its feet. A fleeting image of a Bushman family sitting around a desert fire of their own crossed my mind and brought a smile.

After we had eaten, the tenor of the group changed subtly. Some sat quietly, drawing patterns in the sand with twigs or fingers. Others leaned together, sharing confidences. A dusty dog snuffled from ankle to ankle until someone scratched her back. We spoke in German, their words flowing fluidly while I, my German long unused, struggled to grasp their finer points.

Every now and then one of the men would rise, select a stick and add it to the fire. Just one or two, not enough to make anyone retreat as the flames rose, not enough to waste the wood. Camel thorn acacia is one of Africa's best cooking and heating woods. Hard enough to dull a chisel or blunt an axe, it barely smokes when burned yet produces intense coals that still hold heat enough in the morning to be rekindled with a twist of grass, a twig and a puff of breath. The people of the Namib praise this tree for its evening fires, as well as for its seedpods, an emergency, protein-rich animal feed in the midst of drought.

Later, the coals now coated with ash, they worried about what was on every mind, their futures and that of their children. As minority whites, could they remain with dignity in black-ruled Namibia? The recent, disastrous, racially-inflamed land expropriations in Zimbabwe frightened everyone. Could they keep their farms and ranches in the face of the crescendo occurring locally in land politics? Our analysis crafted in Windhoek detailed the full range of values to be had from this desiccated land, and what land uses would best enhance the welfare of all Namibians. Equally important were sustainability concerns. What high value land uses would preserve the land and water resources, sustaining livelihoods for both blacks and whites, now and through time? That night, we all hoped our recommendations might contribute to a win–win compromise.

We could not have predicted the end result that night. But now, with nearly two decades of hindsight, Namibia's land policy contains nearly every one of the policies we designed that week. Commercial agriculture under private rather than socialized or collectivized ownership thrives. Government's intervention in agriculture remains minimal. No land expropriation has yet occurred. Instead land rights change hands through an open market of willing buyer – willing seller. And government's food policy is one of food security instead of food self sufficiency, allowing land to be put to its highest and best economic use rather than force it to grow corn or millet in places where these are marginal crops at best.

The conversation turned then to the essentials of living in a desert. Rain – always Rain – scanty, precious Rain. A bank of clouds, seen 100 miles to the northwest, raised hope that the dry season might soon end. And if it rained, how would the game adapt? Where would hunters find their quarry? The men recalled a large kudu antelope I had killed a year ago and relived the hunt in detail. Two leopards seen in the vicinity only yesterday brought speculation and some worry. Were there enough baboons in the higher rocky clefts to feed them, or would they come down to the plains looking for someone's flock of goats?

I stood up slowly and walked away to let them talk without me for a while. I found another acacia nearby and settled down against its gnarled trunk, watching just the flow, not specifics any more. Distance blurred the conversation into background music, a stream of words coursing over rocks and pebbles, making tiny bubbly torrents and quiet deeper eddies.

I found myself transported to another time, millennia past. Maybe on this same spot, perhaps nearby, another group might have gathered around camel thorn flames and sat here on the red-brown sands. Neither black nor white, but a diminutive race all their own, they would have been yellow-brown, wizened by the sun. They spoke with the strong clicks and soft vowels of their San Bushmen language. "First People" we call them now, for when they wandered into this vast region, they were entirely alone. They too called this desert home.

Around their evening fire they would have talked of vital things, of game and rains and how to hunt, those elements that mattered most in their struggle for survival. They would have spoken of giant eland bulls, Africa's largest antelope, and acted out their hunts, for they revered the eland and the sustenance it brought them. They would have also talked of leopards, in reverent fear. And in their quiet fireside conversation, these people of the sands renewed their ties with their special God, that spirit who filled their arid home with all that gave them life, drew them together, and sustained their roaming band. I think they saw His footprint in the stars.

A question crept in from the shadows of my mind, lingering there unanswered. In the thirty thousand years or so since the First People arrived, has man discovered new horizons, evolved a new and better self? Or do we struggle now to rediscover truths and ways of being that we knew so clearly way back then?

Some say our human capacity for reason sprang from tracking skills such as the Bushman's, from survival's acute need to stretch the sighting of a single spoor or broken frond into some idea of where the next meal was hiding. Others propose that our species survived only because we clumped together in bands, our earliest communities. I wondered if fire's power to pull us toward one spot helped build the emotional bonds that now unite us. Our bedrock capacities for empathy, compassion, and altruism are rarely found among the other animals. Driven by the need to look out for each other, to share, and to care for the weak, our species divided tasks by gender and age, allowing us to specialize in selected arts of daily living. And this sustained us against the odds.

Perhaps we don't need a Bushman's skills any more. We don't need to be able to smell a leopard, and thus alerted, to forge our keener sight. An antelope's speed no longer hones our muscles or our endurance in the chase. We substitute reason and its first born son, technology, for physical capacities we once had. Ties to the land and to each other, once annealed by fire and ice, made unbreakable by survival's needs, are discarded or never learned. So, the question is, without the constant whetstone of survival's needs, don't the senses atrophy? And what about our spirit, once so tightly bound to the land which gives us life.

For a long moment I was caught within this reverie, trying to guess, across so many boundaries, how the San had understood their land and what it meant to them. What would it have been like to live wholly within a wild environment, in total symbiosis, as but one of myriad species, each with no control over the dynamics of nature? Isn't this the very definition of "wild," the total absence of controls by mankind?

"An area where the earth and its community of life are untrammeled by man," in the words of the Wilderness Act of 1964. It seemed hopeless. Although I could try, I could pretend, I would never be completely like them, so wholly part of the land, immersed in its living rhythms, attuned to its lessons. I could not escape a profound sense of loss.

As I watched, my friend sitting on the ground across the circle reached out, spread his hand wide and slid his fingers deep into the cooling sand. Just behind his hand, the camel thorn also spread roots down into that same sand, reaching deep for the moisture of life. It seemed to me at that moment that our ties with the land may be different now, but, for the lucky few, those ties remain intimate and alive. Like the camel thorn acacia, the men and women with roots in Namib sands are part of their environment, hardened in ways, softened in others, subsumed into the desert itself.

Halfway to the dawn, when the last jackal spread his lonely vocal challenge across the night, with the leopards and the kudu and the rain that waited over the horizon now part of each person's current world, we sought our separate beds. Souls restored, lives filled for now, ties renewed with each other and with the desert, we would take this land's tomorrow as it comes.

Designed to Fail

After a seemingly endless flight, my plane descended toward Islamabad. United from Denver to JFK, Pan Am 001 to Karachi, then Pakistan International Airlines north across 1000 miles of irrigated Sindh and Punjab provinces to the nation's capital. Eighteen groaning hours of travel time. Too much coffee. Food made of cardboard and grease. Little sleep. I was numb except for my gut, which hurt.

For several years, a multi-disciplinary Colorado State University team studied Pakistan's one million miles of earthen irrigation ditches asking how well they delivered water to farmers. We found abysmal conditions. Ditch banks were sponges, shot through with rat holes and root holes and leaking porously. Children bathed the family's water buffalo in the wider spots. Trees, so needed for cooking fuel or fruit, grew in the banks, sucking from the passing flow. Weeds and grasses choked the channels forcing water up and over the banks. Turnouts and diversions leaked. As a result, Pakistan lost nearly half of the water diverted from major rivers before it reached farmers' fields.

Efficiencies after delivery to the edge of a field weren't much better. Farmers irrigated by flooding, cutting holes in the ditch wall and letting water run across their field until the other side was wet, a technique requiring level, or precisely sloped fields. Yet traditional land leveling was little more than dragging a log around behind two bullocks. This often left them with nothing more than hummocks and depressions. Water ponded too deep in the low spots and not deep enough on the high ground. In a single field, crops both drowned and wilted. Overall water losses kept Pakistan on the verge of serious hunger and mired in deep poverty.

Toward the end of my three years on the CSU team, I had pulled together everyone's research, sketched out detailed solutions and wrote a paper estimating the economics of cutting these losses. Benefits far exceeded costs. And aside from simple monetary values, eliminating hunger could be of incalculable value from both political and humanitarian perspectives. We had concluded that managing and maintaining an improved watercourse fell within the skills and capabilities of the average village if they just had some training and if an outside donor would pay for the initial investment to restore ditches to a better standard. USAID and the World Bank committed to putting the answers in place and had asked me back to finish designing a collaborative nationwide action program.

Somewhere over the Atlantic I got to thinking. It had been nearly two years since I was last in Pakistan. Would anyone still be at post in the USAID Mission that I had worked with before? Someone who knew the logic behind our recommendations and would help push them through to approval? Anyone with whom I could talk in that intimate language, the lexicon of colleagues who had been through a couple of years of discovery together in a unique foreign setting?

This was more than just a passing interest. Over the 30 years I had worked in and around USAID as a contractor, I concluded that the Agency had three structural or procedural flaws that essentially prevented full blown success in their development projects. Rapid staff turnover was one of them.

At some past moment, in a burst of infinite wisdom, our foreign service decided that official Americans should not remain at post more than two tours, each of which is normally two years. You may renew once but then you expect to move on to your next country or to a Washington assignment. I once asked why. My State Department friend told me it was to ensure that foreign service personnel did not get too cozy with "the locals. 'Going native,' we call it."

"There is a risk," he said, "that officers who stay at one post too long might become too sympathetic with the host country nationals."

"Is that so wrong?" I asked. "I thought we came over here to understand our hosts and help them out with some of their problems. Getting close to them seems essential if we are doing our job well." He probably thought my question naive, or just plain dumb.

"Our first priority over here is to represent American interests," he replied. "It doesn't happen often, but there have been cases where embassy or USAID personnel had to be sent home because they lost sight of that fact."

* * *

Manzoor Khan, a USAID driver, collected me from the airport. At one time I had suggested they retire him. His reaction time had slowed with age and I, for one, worried every time I rode with him on long trips. Traffic on the major highways was nothing short of nightmarish. Moving hazards ranged from speeding limousines to blaring, careening busses to plodding ox carts filled fifteen feet high with straw. A younger driver with quick reflexes and perfect eyesight seemed essential.

"*Salaam-o-Alaikum, Manzoor Sahib,*" I said. (Peace be upon you.) No need not to be friendly. In the past, Manzoor had often taken me on field trips deep into the Punjab. With his full gray beard, he looked exactly like an *imam* which undoubtedly greased our entry into mud huts and intense conversations.

"I thought you retired."

"No, Sahib. But I only drive in town now. Two more years and I can have my pension."

"Then what will you do?" I asked.

"I go back to my village. My village is in Hazara district. I have a small farm there with apple trees and pears. I will sit and watch my trees and my grand children."

"Then *Insha'Allah* (God willing), I will come visit you and we can both sit and enjoy your apples."

"*Insha'Allah* I will have many apples and we will sit a long time."

Our rapport resurfaced quickly, effortlessly, almost as though we had never been apart. I asked who was still at post in the Mission's agricultural office. Other than Richard Newberg, the chief agricultural officer, Manzoor didn't know any other names. The drivers, he knew, but not the big shots. Maybe my colleagues had all left for other posts, or for "the land of the round doorknobs" as the US was then known.

Newberg, however, was a good start. He had arrived in Islamabad in time to oversee several years of CSU's water management research. He knew the answers we had found and had been one of our stronger supporters. I would be reporting to him on this consultancy. I also knew that the Mission Director, Joseph Wheeler, had been given an unprecedented third tour in-country. Now closing in on six years, he was the consummate "old Pakistani hand" in the mission and he supported the CSU project totally.

It is true that our Foreign Service personnel overseas are over there, in the final analysis, to advance American interests. However, global geopolitics can alter what we define as national interests abruptly, making a shambles out of any continuity for projects on the ground.

Consider our history of assistance to Pakistan. In the mid-1970s U.S. development assistance to Pakistan rose to more than $300 million annually, probably our largest country program after Israel and Egypt. Then intelligence showed that Pakistan was secretly making nuclear weapons, absolutely prohibited by an amendment to the U.S. Foreign Assistance Act for any aid recipient. Congress picked up on this and assistance to Pakistan was abruptly terminated except for what was already in the pipeline. These funds had trickled off to almost nothing; projects were closing out and people going home when the Russians invaded Afghanistan. Suddenly Pakistan was strategically important, a key proxy in the struggle to contain the Soviet Union. President Carter offered $400 million in aid almost immediately. The Pakistanis sneered, calling it "peanuts." President Reagan upped the ante. When the dust settled, U.S. aid to Pakistan had gone from $300 million a year, to almost zero, to $3 billion in the space of a few months, and Pakistan proceeded with impunity working on their bomb. Priorities had changed, however, and most of the field projects previously in place were not renewed.

Another example, in 1988, the Russians retreated from Afghanistan, in 1989 the Berlin Wall fell and in 1991 the Soviet Union came apart at the seams. The Cold War was over. Foreign assistance priorities did an about face, again. The bulk of U.S. development assistance money was redirected to East Europe with the not-so-veiled goal of moving former socialist states into capitalism and democracy. Most of Africa was left holding its hand out but with no luck. The residual formula for Sub-Saharan Africa, at least those nations of no strategic value anymore, was $7 per capita of USAID funding.

I learned of this policy shift abruptly and with dismay one day in Windhoek, Namibia. I had fallen in love with this arid primitive country, its people, and the wildlife and ecology of the Kalahari and Namib Deserts. It reminded me of my youth in the Arizona desert. I badly wanted to work there for a few years and designed a project which I intended to lead to build an agricultural policy capacity into their Ministry of Agriculture, Forestry and Water. I made an appointment with the American Ambassador to sell the idea. She listened intently.

"Jerry, that sounds like a great idea. Such a project is badly needed here, and given what you and your team accomplished in Lesotho, I'm sure you could make it succeed. Now, if this were Moldova or Uzbekistan, or any of the former East Bloc nations, I could probably get approval and funding fairly quickly. But our funds have been redirected to East Europe. Namibia, like a lot of other places, is now on the formula. As you know, Namibia has only a million people and with our budget set by formula at $7 per capita, we can only cover one major program with one in-country project. And I'm sorry but we have already chosen education, not agriculture."

Another example of the whipsaw effect, but driven by a different dynamic is worth telling. In the 1970s, led by a nucleus of dedicated professionals working overseas, myself included, the practice of farming systems research (FSR) was born. FSR involved several methods of bringing small scale farmers directly into the research and testing process so that the ultimate choice of improved technologies would be immediately applicable on their fields, under their unique conditions.

AID jumped on this band wagon with both feet. FSR projects sprang up across the development landscape. By 1987 or 1988 close to $1.0 billion dollars were allocated or being spent on FSR, much of it in Africa. Then, somewhere in the halls of Washington, an influential Senator said "Enough. We will fund no more of these farming systems projects. From now on, we will only fund projects in 'sustainable agriculture.'" No one quite knew what "sustainable" meant but it was the buzzword of the era, and the Senator prevailed. Beginning in late 1989, farming systems, as a philosophy and a development thrust of considerable potential, shriveled from lack of appropriations and died. Ironically, sustainability remains poorly defined. It has been used by so many people to say so many things that, in effect, it now means nothing.

Obviously, stripped to its core, America's foreign assistance must serve our global strategic goals or domestic political goals first. But this means that humanitarian concerns take a back seat in the competition for resources. Sadly, most university people who hire onto international projects are driven by the belief that they will be doing good things for the disadvantaged and the down trodden. Over time, this schism caused interest on university campuses to wane. Universities that had been well along in internationalizing their curricula and student bodies let this priority lapse. International work, where real people might see a change in their lives, failed to stack up against refereed articles in academic journals when it came time to judge faculty merit and award   salary increments.

Limiting diplomatic and official tours to a four year maximum might not be such an issue were it not those projects usually need longer than that to mature. Herein lies the third structural flaw in the USAID project approach. In a project's Year 1, the project team arrives and settles in, beginning to develop relationships with their local counterparts. Years 2 and 3, then, are when the discovery of solutions, testing for local relevance, and adaptation to on-the-ground realities occurs. Years 4 and 5 see the fleshing out of recommended changes and a shift toward broader applications, taking experimental results off the research station and across the country onto farmers' fields. When institution building is a key project goal, several more years may be needed to entrench new practices, procedures and objectives. Thus, five years is a "normal" project life. Many need to run a decade or longer.

Couple this dynamic with the "two tours and out" rule in USAID and it is almost a certainty that when your project reaches its end, nobody remains in the USAID Mission who was there at the start. Nobody, really, with a vested interest in whether the project succeeds or fails.

A bureaucratic dynamic operates here as well to make things worse. Careers of Mission Directors are made by one of two processes; either the amount of assistance funding to the host country increases dramatically under the Director's watch or his tenure launched a new and imaginative program initiative. Trajectories for the flow of funds to a particular nation are largely set in Washington, heavily influenced by Congress, and Congressional politics, so this route to career advancement is rare.

Imaginative new program thrusts work like this. A career officer learns she is to become Mission Director in Country X and will be departing to post in, say, three months. She flies over there for an orientation, a set of briefings, and a look-around to see what she might do that is new and interesting. Something to put her stamp on the overall program in this new country of her's. Assume for illustration that this visit starts the programming clock that will characterize her success or failure at post. This is T-0. She comes back home with her new idea and commits some serious desk time to drafting up the paperwork and floating the idea up and down the halls of the appropriate branch of AID/Washington. For this illustration, assume she decides her grand new idea needs a university contractor for its ability to provide scientific research support to the field team and graduate degrees to their counterparts. Assume also that a University A is already in-country, under contract, diligently working on their own project which was designed by the previous Mission Director. Assume they are half-way through their own Year 3, that point at which tangible benefits should start to flow.

At T+3 (counting in months) she departs for her new assignment with Washington's blessings for her new program thrust. Shortly after landing, she assembles the in-country staff and they start work on a Project Paper (the PP). This may or may not require a 2-3 day visit by program designers from Washington. If they hurry, at T+6 they have a document

209

fleshed out well enough to send to AID/Washington for an in-concept approval. Discussions around the coffee pot in-country are beginning to focus on the Director's new idea. Some folks imagine a coattail effect dragging their own careers along if this really takes off.

Once Washington approves the concept, (T+8) things really get rolling. The Mission gears up to produce a very detailed Project Identification Document (PID). Usually this entails a 2-3 week in-country visit by a team of consultants. Finding the consultants, briefings, organization and logistics adds 4-5 weeks up front. Since the PID details day to day activities, goals and sub-goals, relationships between the contractor team and local professionals, the host government must be intensively involved. It is rare for a PID process to be completed in-country and approved in Washington in less than four months. Six is more likely, bringing us to T+14.

Having full approval by AID/Washington actually means little until Congress has appropriated the funds. This process can take between two months and forever. Let's optimistically assume three months, taking us to T+17. If the bureaucrats have been doing their homework in advance, the Request for Proposal (RFP) has been drafted and now awaits Congressional action. The RFP will be released through the Commerce Business Daily newspaper and other media with a two month deadline for responses. T+19. A meeting in Washington of prospective bidders convenes. Bids come in, usually at the last possible minute just because that's the way universities work. A short list of three bidders emerges. Then the host country sends one or more senior administrators to the U.S. joining AID folks in site visits where each finalist presents their best case for the project. Add two months, reaching T+21.

The successful bidder is announced. Let's call it University B. On campus, high-fives are slapped, celebratory libations quaffed. However, final selection of the field team and their orientation to the project and their new home overseas can take some time. Also, assembling 3 or 5 or 8 university professionals, their families, and all their household effects and getting them across an ocean, housed and settled into their new home is a six month process minimum. I've done it several times.

We have now arrived at T+27 on the Director's programming clock. She is just starting her second *and last* two-year tour and she is in a hurry to make this thing work. All attention now focuses on the new program. Staff in the Mission is fully engaged in getting the Director's initiative off to a great start. University B is in place ready to go. From the perspective of the host government, there are new computers, lab equipment and other toys to play with, new field vehicles to drive, new short course and degree scholarships to be had. Whatever directorate of the Ministry hosts this project is now showered with attention. The Honorable Minister arrives in his chauffeured black Mercedes to officially welcome the new team and inaugurate the project.

Meanwhile, across the dusty parking lot, maybe even in the same Ministry, University A's team is now only three months away from their EOP (end of project) date. Will they get a project extension? Probably not. Most of the Mission's budget is now directed to other priorities built around the University B project. Remember, no one in the USAID office today took part in the design, implementation and early nurturing of University A's work. Will there be an End of Project Evaluation. Yes. Congress mandates one, but no one will likely ever read it. Will the practical lessons they learned be transmitted to the new guys? Not unless the two Chiefs of Party know each other socially from somewhere in the past. Will the host government carry on their work? Not likely. All the new chances for promotions, salary enhancements, study trips with international per diem, scholarships for degrees abroad now lie with the new project. Gradually, the better, more eager officers will trickle into this new point of dynamism, expecting to get in on all the action. Their positions will be back-filled with civil servants of lower energy levels, less education, and fewer political connections.

Five years down the road, when University B finds itself wondering why they can't get a project extension, why all their best trained local staff have taken other positions, there will not likely be tangible evidence anywhere that University A was ever there.

Trail's End

Because South Africa segregated its universities by race, the American Fulbright program boycotted them for decades. In 1991 a new ambassador, Bill Swing, rewrote that policy. Swing reasoned that we might influence change more effectively from within a net of collegial academic contacts than simply standing outside hurling invective. When the program reopened, I jumped at the chance and became the first Fulbright Professor into South Africa in over 20 years. My research topic for the award was, "Economic Policies for a Post-Apartheid South Africa." The University of Cape Town, School of Economics, made me welcome as a Fulbright Professor with essentially carte blanche to get on with my research. The Development Bank of Southern Africa liked what this research might produce and provided a desk in their Centre for Policy Analysis, some expert colleagues, and domestic travel support in the form of air fare and per diem.

Working with colleagues from the Prime Minister's office, the Development Bank and UCT, I used the Social Accounting Matrix (SAM) I had developed with Davie Mullins and our team to evaluate a series of growth strategies built around egalitarianism, income redistribution and an end to poverty. Whites feared income redistribution thinking that black gains could only come at the expense of white losses, effectively a zero sum game. However, the South African SAM proved that new black purchasing power, if they ever got any, would soon bubble up to white owned businesses that supplied products and raw materials, increasing jobs, wages and profits in those sectors. In fact, it was a win-win situation. It was also clear from the model that added incomes received by whites rarely "trickled down" to lower income levels. Economic theory in this regard was false and we could prove it.

We were suggesting not only policy changes but also a new attitude toward other races. White South Africa was having trouble turning loose of past beliefs and embracing the sweeping changes that were obviously coming. To accelerate their grasp of an inevitable future, I criss-crossed the country as a one-man dog and pony show trying to enlighten anyone who would listen. I called my presentation "Scenario I" because, in my view, it was the only peaceful way forward. I addressed universities, business leaders, Cabinet officers, politicians, trade groups and labor unions, over twenty presentations in all. I even went clandestinely to Botswana, crossing the border on a tourist visa, to meet with the exiled Pan Africanist Congress of Azania, and its armed wing, to talk about moderate economic policies. That trip was an eye-opener. Many of the T-shirts in the crown that week advocated, "One Settler – One Bullet." Revolutionary rhetoric of the day labeled whites as settlers, asserting that blacks had arrived first and accordingly this was their land to be reclaimed at the point of a gun.

By then it was obvious to me that the African National Congress (ANC) would be the next government and Nelson Mandela, most likely the next president. It seemed logical to make my pitch to the ANC's economic development policy personnel. If I could talk the white guys into accepting blacks into the mainstream, maybe I could talk the black guys into letting the whites stay in this country with dignity too. Down any other path there could be much blood spilled.

I called Max Sisulu, the ANC director of development policy, wrangled an invite, and flew to Joburg to give my pitch. For the first time, I ran into a vitriolic buzz saw of angry opposition. The ANC economic development staff loudly chastised me for ignoring their history of misery, for not redressing the fact they had been deprived of their land at the point of a gun, and for relying on white owned capitalism to create black jobs. I was, they charged, "a-historical," and "out of touch with the realities of The Struggle." They demanded nationalization of industry, adopting some extreme variant of socialism, and punitive treatment of white South Africans. Not quite "one settler – one bullet" but close. Much of the noise, surprisingly, came from young extremist Brits, mostly white, Jewish and über-liberal, who had attached themselves to the ANC. As we walked out to the car, Max apologized for my treatment. He had been embarrassed.

It turned out that Max was not without some clout within the ANC. His father, Walter Sisulu had spent two decades imprisoned on Robben Island with Mandela, refining their vision of a perfect South Africa. A triumvirate; Nelson Mandela, Walter Sisulu, and Govan Mbeki, stood atop the ANC leadership pantheon. Their vision would shape this country. Max must have said something to his dad about the behavior of his economic policy staff for within a month the whole lot of them had been sent abroad "for further studies." I found it all very interesting.

Within a few weeks, Thabo Mbeki, Govan's son, who was presumed to be the future Foreign Minister, secretly visited the Development Bank. Secretly, because the ANC's public posture forbade discussions with any branch of the white government. He met with Simon Brand, the Bank's Director General and my ping-pong adversary at Stanford, and asked for help designing economic policies for the ANC that the foreign community might accept. Thabo admitted that the ANC didn't have their own economists who could get it right. They were all abroad doing their "further studies."

After Thabo's visit the question came down from upstairs, relayed by Nick Vink, head of the Centre for Policy Analysis where I worked.

"Can you do it?" Simon wanted to know.

"I think so," I answered. "I've got a pretty good start already with my Scenario I speech." We agreed that Nick and Lolette, another Development Bank colleague, would join and our team of three would adapt my scenario speech.

Then, like another Director General in Lahore, Pakistan, Simon asked, "How soon can you start?" To which he added, "Can you have it done in three weeks?" Finally, "There can be no identification as to who wrote this or where it came from. This must be an ANC document." Three weeks later, Thabo Mbeki returned for his document and I gave him a sixty minute briefing on the benefits of income redistribution and poverty reduction, ways the ANC might accomplish that and the sweeping implications possible for South Africa.

Thabo had brought an associate with him, an inflexible revolutionary, who seemed unwilling to accept anything we said. We were, in his eyes, "the enemy," As I was closing the briefing, he disdainfully interjected, "We haven't heard anything here today that we didn't already know." Thabo turned to him coolly and said, "Why don't you wait outside."

The associate blanched, if that is possible for a very dark black man, and silently retreated to sit with the receptionist in the outer room. Thabo turned to me and asked, "Is there anything else you have for me?"

It was a once-in-a-lifetime moment. Five minutes, maybe ten, to dip an oar into the current of history. I dropped all caution and told Thabo Mbeki what I felt were essential changes in the ANC's political stance. It was crucial, I said, that the ANC rein in the rabid pro-communist fomentations of its youth wing, and its leader at that time, Winnie Mandela, if they were to join the international community as respected partners. I was way out on a limb here. Winnie was Nelson's estranged wife. I mentioned her by name, nonetheless. I thought she threatened the country's future.

"Do you know what you are suggesting?" he asked when I mentioned Mrs. Mandela.

"Yes, I do." A long pause hung there between us.

I told him that I thought they also needed to wean their political stance away from the demands of the South African Communist Party (SACP) which wanted to socialize much of the private sector. This also was a risky position. The fight for freedom in South Africa had rested on a three-legged political stool, the Tripartite Alliance they called it. The SACP was one of those legs. Finally I weighed in on the most vigorous economic debate at the time, "empowerment" vs. "entitlement." Entitlement advocates felt that the ruling whites had kept the blacks suppressed for so long and so viciously that they were entitled to redress. Practically, this boiled down to plans for expropriating white resources, their jobs, their land and most everything else, and reallocating these to blacks. I knew the white population well enough to know that civil war lay down that path and I told him so. Empowerment was more akin to affirmative action and thus more likely to be accepted by the white electorate. Empowerment meant "Give me the skills and resources and open up opportunities for me to use them." The world community would like that. I think I took more than ten minutes, but Thabo listened carefully. It was an open, two-way discussion, not a harangue.

I know that the ANC was hearing many of these points from across the spectrum of people they talked to. The international community delivered some of these points directly to Mandela, particularly the emphasis on a private sector economy rather than socialism, at the annual conference in Davos, Switzerland. However, I did find it interesting that within weeks, Mrs. Mandela was stripped of much of her leadership role in ANC dialogue.

Mbeki never became Foreign Minister. Instead, he succeeded Mandela as the country's second President, serving two terms of his own. Some weeks after our meeting in Pretoria, I was at home in Cape Town when the phone rang. On the other end, in an excited voice, Nick Vink urged me to turn on the television. Thabo Mbeki was announcing to a national ANC policy conference the final results of their policy deliberations. ANC members from communities across the country had spent a week of populist democracy debating and crafting policies on a wide range of topics including population, health, technology, education, and others. Results of this conference were to become the foundations of the party's main platform themes during and after election. As my TV flickered to life, he was announcing the ANC's new economic policy. I stood there, transfixed. Chapter and verse,

Thabo Mbeki was reading straight from my document. Once the ANC took office, those recommendations emerged as the underpinnings of the Reconstruction and Development Programme, the centerpiece of Nelson Mandela's first economic program.

Later that night, I poured myself a glass of one of South Africa's best red wines and sat before a fire of grape vine prunings, musing over the roller coaster ride it had all been. Like that stroll through my experimental plots in Faizalabad, accompanied by the ringing call to evening prayer, when I knew Pakistan's agricultural research had been changed forever and for the better. Like the night in Pretoria after the SAM meeting, when I knew the country could never again ignore the income inequality that blighted it. This moment was another one, filled with indefinable feelings, almost an out of body moment. Honestly, I felt like I was floating up there just under my Cape Dutch thatched ceiling, looking down on myself in front of that fire. In that moment, everything had come together and I just knew something right had happened.

My reflections brought up all those who made it work. Phil Austin, president at CSU and P.W. Botha, Prime Minister of South Africa, each of whom had the courage to say "Go For It, I'll cover your back." The two Director Generals in their very disparate settings, who trusted a foreigner to change their countries. There were those who didn't make it to see the end, if there ever can be an end, who gave their lives to their commitment: Manapo Moshoeshoe, His Majesty King Moshoeshoe II, Victor Ntsekhe, Simon Brand and others. And then there were my incredible "constellations of comets," three in all. The Ford Foundation Green Revolution team in

Pakistan with their collection of Nobel and national prize winners, each justly honored. The group of technical buddies under Dawie Mullins' leadership who built the largest, most powerful SAM ever for Africa with its detailed emphasis on individuals by race and income level. And the gang at the Development Bank of Southern Africa, led by Nick Vink and, before his untimely death, Simon Brand, who put ethics on the table for discussion and struggled hard to find and fund myriad ways forward toward the New South Africa we all hoped for.

And I remembered my Pakistani office mate, Jiri Prazak and those three crumpled yellow sheets of paper in a colonial office dustbin in Lahore. Such a tiny innocuous start with such gigantic impacts. To no one in particular, and to all of them together, I silently lifted my glass and fervently said "Thank you! It's been one helluva ride my friends."

Part IV: Random Moments in the Kaleidoscope of Forty Years

Last Shot

Izaak, the Herero tracker, had seen it first. His practiced eyes caught spots in the grass that didn't seem to belong there, and then a softly curved line of muscle that had to be feline. Knuckles tapped code on the truck's cab roof – two taps – Stop Quick. Brakes caught, small showers of gravel splayed from under each tire. Standing in the pickup's open bed, Izaak and I were thrown against the gun rack at the front. Our commotion flushed a brace of guinea fowl. Half a mile away, a troop of baboons watched. When our sound reached them, a big hoary male barked a warning from his lookout perch in a towering acacia and forty black specks scurried for cover. Helmut, professional hunting guide, good friend and owner of this Namibian game ranch, clambered out of the cab. Urgently Izaak whispered *gepard*, cheetah in German, and pointed. Two hundred yards beyond his reaching finger stood the animal, half hidden in grass that nearly touched its shoulder, staring at us. We had disturbed its morning nap.

Helmut drew a deep breath. "Jerry, Shoot it. Shoot! It kills my goats." I grabbed my rifle from the rack in the bed of the pickup, clicked the bolt back and jammed it forward, chambering a round. I looked for the cat in the scope, only to see it bolt. In that moment, I didn't think. With practiced reflex, skills honed in a lifetime of hunting took over.

I followed it in the cross hairs as it leaped away when Izaak became very excited in his Herero language. Helmut spit out a "*Mein Gott!*" and instantly changed instructions. "Not that little one, Jerry. There. That big one. Shoot! *Ach, mein Gott.*" Where the first cheetah had stood, seen us and run, a much larger cheetah now rose slowly from its bed, leaned forward to stretch and turned his head our way. His lithe body froze, thigh muscles sculpted by slanting sunlight. Penetrating yellow eyes examined us; characteristic black tear marks outlined its muzzle. The grass only came up to this one's belly.

We were hunting Greater Kudu, to my mind Africa's most beautiful antelope. This very large cheetah now in my cross hairs was an accident of location and timing, our random paths intersecting on this hillside of dried grass and scattered thorn bush. We had not even thought of crossing paths with a cheetah. However, in Namibia, taking a livestock-killing cheetah is legal, and this cat killed Helmut's goats. Adrenaline took over. I took half a breath, held it, settled the cross hairs and fired. One shot. Its roar violating the savannah silence. That great cheetah flinched, then vaulted forward. It took two jumps and collapsed in a tumble behind a stunted thorn bush.

We approached carefully. He had been hit but we didn't know how badly. I stole to within 20 feet before I saw him, just his ears and glaring eyes crouched low in the grass. Our eyes met. The grasses between us twitched. Suddenly, he exploded straight at me, a blur of spotted hide, parting grasses and scattered gravel. Instinctively, with no time to aim, I raised my rifle butt as a club. He dodged around my legs, springing first left, then right. His long tail slapped against my thigh. He was desperate and dying, wanting only escape. Two more jumps, he collapsed again, and it was over.

226

Or was it? Now, a suffocating silence blanketed that hillside. As if something were missing. As if that cheetah had taken something vital with him into death.

This cheetah, the male of the pair, was huge, bigger than most full-grown leopards. Helmut and Izaak bubbled with excitement over its size. We honored the moment with ageless German hunting rituals. We placed a sprig of green foliage, the ceremonial "Last Bite," in the animal's mouth. *"Weidmannsheil,"* said Helmut, praise to the hunter. *"Weidmannsdank,"* I replied in thanks. Shot glasses and some very cold schnapps appeared. We toasted the big cat. We toasted Izaak. The others raised their glasses in toast to my incredible luck and to me. I found myself watching, as though from a distance, as if it were happening to someone else. Inside, I could feel a small dark spot growing. Something hollow.

* * *

When I started hunting, I swore I would never kill one of the big cats. To me they were special, and I understood their generally threatened status. I lived by that choice for half my life, hunting various deer and antelope species, each threatened more by their own overpopulation than by scarcity. Now what had I done? As the adrenaline subsided, I walked back to the bush under which my "trophy" lay. But I saw no cheetah. I saw a crumpled pile of blood-smeared spotted hide, one long leg jutting skyward and two eyes still open, seeing nothing.

Many hunters long for a record book entry. At one time, I had as well. I almost made it into the Boone and Crockett *Records of North American Big Game* with a Sonoran whitetail deer from southern Arizona. Now here I was in Africa, home of Rowland Ward's *Records of Big Game*, the international listing, and I had just shot a very large cheetah. Later, although still numbed by it all, I asked Helmut if his diminutive Bushman skinner could take extra care with the skull so that it might be measured. Perhaps Rowland Ward would honor this magnificent animal.

My cheetah ranks as the 32nd largest ever recorded in 110 years of Rowland Ward records. However, I find neither joy nor pride in this and I don't speak of it often. The statistic does the cheetah no justice. He lived a life unknown, never lauded, except perhaps for those ten seconds when he rose slowly from his savannah bed and looked my way. That scene remains branded on my memory; supple muscles stretching, riveting eyes stock still above waving grass, an image of feline tranquility and sublime wild power.

His death is recorded differently as a single line in a book filled with of 717 pages of them. It's not an honor role, nor a listing of merit. It's just an obituary, reduced to nothing but inches of skull bone, for that is all that remains of him.

Length: 7 ½
Width: 5 ⅛
Total: 12 ⅝
Locality: Windhoek, Namibia
Date: 1991
Owner: Professor Jerry B. Eckert

Three sets of eyes evaluated my cheetah that day. Such an ironic term, "my cheetah," as if by extinguishing something, one possesses it. Izaak's saw proof that his game scouting skills remained sharp as ever. Helmut saw a spectacular trophy produced on his farm, by his team. I saw what many would consider the chance of a lifetime turn into gnawing questions.

There must have been a fourth pair of eyes that day. Crouched on a not too distant hillside, I believe his mate was watching. In her eyes there would have been fear, her peace shattered by the rifle's roar. I wonder now if there might have been something else as well. Could there have been anguish?

Helmut ordered the live trap brought up from the ranch and baited. To protect his goats, the female would be trapped and moved to a national game preserve. A large steel frame and chain link cage arrived with a heavy trap door. The bait? Pieces of the male's hide, his guts and some blood. "She will come," Helmut asserted from experience. "They always return to their mate."

We found her there at daybreak, caged. Her muzzle and fore paws crouched low over her mate's remains, as if protecting the few pieces she had left, snarling in defiance. There was terror in her eyes. Or maybe hate? I really couldn't tell. As I drew near, she lunged with a roar, straight for my throat, stopped only by iron bars and steel mesh. I recoiled, panicked for an instant.

* * *

Old passions die hard, especially this hunting life, so central it is to who I am. My grandpa taught me hunting and wilderness skills beginning with a trap line we ran together over the Christmas holiday in 1950. While we tramped his snow-draped woods checking our sets for rabbits, he told me his stories of Ohio's rural culture of 1900, the year he settled that farm and fed his new bride fresh meat caught with those very same traps in those same woods. Through him, while running our trap line, I came to know of a horse-drawn agriculture, complete with wood cookstoves, squirrel stew and biscuits, hogs butchered in November, Jersey cows milked by hand on icy February mornings.

A generation later, the best times I ever had with my father were when, rifles in hand, we hunted roe and red deer in Germany, whitetail and mulies in the United States. In Germany, we embraced the centuries-old traditions that venerate the game and its pursuit, and elevate hunting to an honorable endeavor. It seemed that only when in the forest on the hunt could my father, the diplomat, relax and be both himself and my friend, that father that I loved best.

The first time I hunted without him marked my passage to full adulthood, a final emancipation at age 20. I camped alone on that hunt beside some bear scat, 6,800 feet up on a pinyon-juniper ridge of an Arizona mountain. With my favorite rifle, the one my dad gave me on my 17th birthday, the rifle I would use in Namibia one day, I worked the lung-bursting high country above, and finally killed a large classically configured Sonoran whitetail buck.

Jose Ortega y Gasset, the Spanish philosopher-hunter, famously defined the hunter as the "alert man," suggesting an intense connection with nature found only in hunting. I think he defined me for I have felt that intensity in my gut. I am never more whole than when I am deep inside a wilderness. I am never more attuned to that wilderness, its every shadow, every leaf fall, the slightest spoor, every squirrel's scolding chatter, than when I prowl there, transformed for a short while into man – the predator.

So, I cannot disparage hunting or the hunters who do it well and with conscience. I wish them all a *Weidmannsheil*. As for me, however, I simply cannot forget Helmut's words, "They always return to their mate." Nor the fury of a cheetah's lunge at me from inside that cage. As though she knew who had pulled the trigger.

That night, I cleaned my Winchester Model-70, .30-06, with its classic walnut stock, my trusted field companion of nearly 40 years, and slid her slowly into her sheepskin-lined carrying case, where she remains to this day, untouched.

Publish or Perish

My flight home for Christmas with my family should have been filled with happy anticipation. Yet, something had nagged at me as I crossed the Atlantic. January 1st loomed just ahead, the date we academics count up our accomplishments for our annual performance rating. We each dutifully list our teaching, research and service achievements, being careful not to exaggerate enough so that we get caught, and submit our lists to a committee of our peers. We know full well that only research publications count for much despite the administration's passionate fulminations about teaching students. If we excel, a larger than average salary increment is awarded. If we fall short, a reduced or nonexistent increment follows along with scalding words from the department head.

I already knew I was in trouble. I had spent the whole year leading a research team in Pretoria working on an economic approach to ending apartheid peacefully. Unfortunately, at Colorado State University, this type of work is labeled "service," and ranked even lower than teaching in performance calculations. I knew when I started the job in Pretoria that there would be a tradeoff. Writing in the style and voice that persuades nations to change almost guarantees the work will be rejected by academic journals. So I made a choice, and I would do it all over again if needed. I was already a tenured full professor, so they could not fire or promote me, only adjust my salary. And ending apartheid was more important to me than the size of my salary increment.

On my accomplishments list this year, I could show a written output of 250,000 words, published in reports accepted by South Africa's Prime Minister, printed and distributed widely under his order. My year's high point was a national conference, convened by the Prime Minister's Office, to formally place our results into their national policy dialogue. But, despite that conference having turned our work into the economic currency of the time, despite the fact that South Africa's trajectory out of apartheid was now clear, irreversible and accelerating, I had no articles in academic journals to show for my year. 1,500 words in the American Economic Review would have counted far more in the eyes of the departmental committee. The "System" was about to punish me.

Sitting in a passenger lounge in JFK that December night, frustration boiled over into rebellion. Maybe it was my bitterness over the reduced performance rating and punitive salary increment I would soon receive. Or maybe I finally saw academic priorities for what they really are. My profession's emphasis on journal articles suddenly seemed like an inane irrelevancy. Carried to its logical end, as it often is, it can destroy marriages, social lives, careers, even one's health. I was reminded of something written by an enlightened academic whose name I have now forgotten, "A person's true worth is not measured on his or her résumé."

"I'll show those bastards." With ten hours to kill before an onward flight to Denver, I would use them to draft a totally fictitious article that I might slip past some journal referees, those gate keepers to the academic pantheon, and expose

The System for what it really was. Around midnight, I found a deserted coffee shop with a quiet table in the corner, pulled out a lined tablet and pen, and set about writing a publishable journal article without a shred of truth in it. Lots of colorful verisimilitude. Realistic, believable, faux Africana. But total fiction.

I needed a bogus theory as my centerpiece. Like most economic theories, mine should express a common sense principle obfuscated with fifty dollar words, like "obfuscate," a theory which allowed academics to quibble over nuances important only to them. Something with a crushing impact on no one in particular. And I had a real case study in mind, an African nation that expelled a team of foreign experts rather than accept the truth of their findings. This secret bit of African history led me to the most basic formula of all, how to calculate an arithmetic average, something we all learn by third grade.

First, I needed some hypothetical scientists to quibble with each other. Back in the eighth grade, while studying Spanish and Arizona history in the same semester, the surname of an early explorer fascinated me. What was it like to go through life named Head of a Cow? Álvar Núñez Cabeza de Vaca's main claim to fame was walking from the site of his ship wreck in Florida to Mexico City, arriving almost naked after seven years, and along the way being the first European to hear from the Indians of the fabled Seven Golden Cities of Cibola. Since everyone, or at least someone, might remember Cabeza de Vaca as an explorer, I couldn't give him a lead role in my fable. I needed another, equally improbable surname and settled on a Germanic equivalent, Schweinkopf, or "Pig Head."

Professor Schweinkopf, I wrote, originated the theory that the formula for an arithmetic mean, an average to most of us, only works if the results are politically meaningless. I also gave the Cow's Head his moment in the sun, writing that Professor Cabeza de Vaca's quantitative work first proved and then extended Schweinkopf's findings. My title, complete with an erudite subtitle, became, "The Schweinkopf Hypothesis: Empirical Evidence and Refutation." Both the words and structure carried a nice academic ring. The article then began with a first paragraph steeped in full-blown academic-speak, designed to ensure that no one read much further.

Received theory, as pioneered by Schweinkopf (1947) and refined by de Vaca (1952, 1953), stipulates that parametric centrality in social phenomena is fundamentally related to mean behavioral observations. While the general concept was in evidence in several earlier works (Anonymous, 1867; Fou, 1931), it remained for Schweinkopf to postulate the now widely used linear additive model. Then, in a quantitative tour de force, *de Vaca (1952) proved conclusively that the weights implicit in Schweinkopf's model were homogenous of degree zero and homothetic. Finally, de Vaca showed that the use of binary primary data yields unbiased estimates at the limit, n =* ∞.

What's not to like? Homogenous of degree zero, linear additive model, received theory, mean behavioral observations, and parametric centrality, fifty dollar phrases, one and all. "Primary binary data" actually means nothing but it rhymes nicely. In the list of "References" at the end, the 1867 paper by Anonymous was, in true mid-19th Century fashion, titled, *"Intellectual Travels Through Science: Being a Treatise on Behaviors Common to Men and Inanimate Objects, with*

Illustrations by the Author." The cited reference from 1931 was written by Dr. Suis Fou, French for "I'm crazy."

I needed a reason for this article, something that appeared to move the quest for the perfect theory forward. The Schweinkopf Hypothesis needed verification using apparently real African village data. Then I would pitch the whole insoluble quandary into the international academic arena for debate, as so often happens.

Recent data, however, have cast doubt on the immutability of this quantitative relationship, thus questioning its underlying conceptual framework. Instances are emerging in which relationships between observed behavior and known facts vary. While the fragmentary nature of present observations prevents final conclusions, sufficient data exist to suggest that the relationship varies with certain aggregate income measures, particularly GNP per capita, and that the relationship is either non-linear or linear with indiscrete discontinuities.

"Immutability, fragmentary nature, linear with indiscrete discontinuities." I was on a roll.

Now I needed to present the "research" data that brought the issue to a head. But first a credible location, somewhere remote, somewhere no one has ever heard of and thus can't be double checked with World Bank or UN data. I have always loved the name of a little village up-country in The Gambia where my Mixed Farming project worked, only because it sounds so truly African. I shamelessly stole the name, camouflaged its location and gave it several stereotypic African characteristics.

Mansakonko is a small, rural community in north-central southern Africa. Its economy is largely composed of farming and rural trade. Practically the only source of wage employment is the somewhat overstaffed civil service, which

237

draws its entire budget from taxes on land and agricultural products. Primary production is confined to crop and livestock farming, one consequence of which is extreme annual variability in aggregate income. Mansakonko is poor, with mean incomes usually guesstimated at less than $300/capita, the level used by international donor and financing agencies to separate grant from loan recipients. Accordingly, Mansakonko receives its foreign assistance as grants and has only minimal foreign debt.

Now for my case study. I knew of one former British colony that had no estimate of its per-capita income level when they gained independence. This country's leaders invited a World Bank team in to calculate this figure and to develop local capacities to do their own estimates of Gross National Product (GNP) in the future. After nearly a year's work by five expat economic experts, they handed over their answers to government. Unfortunately, they had estimated GNP per person at just above the $300 threshold. If this estimate held up, this very poor nation would have to borrow their development funds from now on, building up their international debt. Outright grants would no longer be available. Relationships with donor nations would change irrevocably.

True story. Within a day or two, the World Bank team learned that their work visas had been revoked. Within a week, they were gone, escorted to the airport by government officials. Within a month, their "flawed measurements" had been revised by the local Bureau of Statistics to show that GNP averaged well below $300 as had always been assumed. Grant funding by donors resumed.

What a perfect case study, I thought. I would fictionalize it a bit, maybe more than a bit, and no one would be the wiser. I wrote up a massive but fictitious rural effort to collect farm production data, modeled closely after our project's field work in Gambia. I added in an American university (like my own) contracted to run the project, gave them ample donor funding (such as we had) and a computer program with the acronym FUMBLE. Field data, I said, were collected using a method developed by an old German farmer, Joachim Bauer. For the title of his "path breaking research," I corrupted Stanford University's motto, "Die Luft der Freiheit Weht" (the winds of change blow,) which is always expressed in German, changing it into "Die Luft der Unsinn Weht," (the winds of nonsense blow,) published presumably in the *German Archives of Unbelievable Research*, all hidden in typically dense German language.

Given the intensive nature of the baseline work, it was feasible to physically enumerate the area of every cropped field in Mansakonko in 1982. Hectarage data were thus available with a closing error of $\pm$ 0.035. Pooled standard error of the estimates fell consistently below three percent. Thus, the data base was as accurate as can be expected under African field conditions. Further, after several years of foreign assistance, including expatriate advisors, participant training, vehicles and other support to field work, the Department of Statistics was widely believed to be among the most proficient in sub-Saharan Africa. Accordingly, the results of Mansakonko's first-ever agricultural production estimates were eagerly awaited. . . . Several permuted distribution functions were tested. Best fit occurred, as expected, using the Schweinkopf-de Vaca model.

Needing a source of conflict or confusion, I split this "most proficient" Bureau of Statistics into a Numerator Section and a Denominator Section. Then I forbade them to talk to each other in the interests of doing their job without outside bias. When each section was done, they independently presented their results to the Prime Minister who praised them both, volubly and publicly. Seeking a bit of local fame, each section also released their numbers to the press. Ever curious, the press put numerator and denominator together and found that GNP/capita was $325, well above the grant/loan threshold. Gasping sounds were heard. Consternation reigned.

To solve this dilemma and add a bit more African flavor I called up the authority of a Paramount Chief, a queen in this case. There were no reigning queens in Sub-Saharan Africa at that time, but who would know?

Mansakonkan society, while in rapid transition to a more Western model, still vests several key responsibilities in the Paramount Chief. Among these are the allocation of land, adjudication of certain disputes, legitimation of marriages and children, divining water and certifying truths. In this latter capacity, Her Majesty, the Paramount Chief, serves as the final authority on questions of fact.

After three weeks reviewing her government's work, this fictional Queen settled the issue by publishing an Edict of Fact, quoted here.

"We have been informed of the exemplary recent work of the staff of the Department of Statistics. We further note that His Excellency, the Right Honourable Prime Minister has accepted with gratitude the recent data released by the Department of Statistics. Therefore, under the authority vested by the Mansakonko Ancestral Code, Section 7-3.B (2)(a), We do hereby affirm the following facts:

(1) Total output for 1982 was 14,392,000 dollars,

(2) Total population in 1982 was 44,283 persons,

(3) Per capita output in 1982 was, therefore, 273 dollars.

Given Under Royal Seal

I had used a fancy formula for the Schweinkopf Hypothesis throughout the paper. The numbers from the Edict of Fact placed into this formula averaged $325 per capita, just as the press had calculated. Not $273 as was now a certified fact. There was only one possible conclusion:

Thus with data of impeccable accuracy and the authority of none other than the Paramount Chief of Mansakonko, the Schweinkopf Hypothesis appears to have been refuted. Certainly it is called into question.

In the real world of foreign assistance, this sort of conundrum might have led to an international conference, lots of experts traveling abroad, meetings near a beach in some Club Med-type facility, renewal of good ol' boy relations and much consumption of imported beer and exotic cuisine. Of course I added all this into my article. I brought old farmer Bauer out of retirement with a very generous consulting fee. But I wanted some new faces, preferably young, intelligent, female academics to put the old fogeys in their place. With their striking individuality implied by their given names, yet with togetherness suggested in their surnames, Drs. Chastity Mudd and Salome Quagmire rose from out of nowhere to dominate the conference. Their jointly authored paper with the impossible title, "Flux in Theoretical Constants" had made them a cause célèbre among statisticians worldwide. They offered their novel theory to the meeting that even the laws of physics decayed with time, suggesting a new type of theoretical entropy.

From the outset, two schools of thought emerged. Conservatives, led by Bauer himself, called for an International Commission of Verification which Mr. Bauer graciously volunteered to lead, provided that his World Bank consulting fee continued. Revisionists, on the other hand, postulated that the only constant was change itself. Building on this hypothesis, Quagmire and Mudd (1984) released their most recent computations which suggested that statistical

241

formulae have half lives of 32.7 years and that the Schweinkopf Hypothesis must therefore be accepted as obsolescent. The conference foundered bitterly on this dichotomy. A resolution was not forthcoming.

As really happened in a certain country I know, the lack of solid evidence to the contrary led to a resumption of grant funding instead of loans. Both the local government and the donor community expressed complete satisfaction with the outcome. Within Mansakonko, those who supported the Queen's numbers were promoted. Those who had erred were sent abroad "for further training."

Like any good researcher, I suggested additional future research and laid out a methodology that would have kept me funded for years. By now, even I was almost believing this story and I really did want to test the Quagmire-Mudd hypothesis with field data. And then there was this postscript:

On the occasion of the twentieth anniversary of the Independence of Mansakonko, the government of that sovereign land unveiled a new national crest. The new design maintained the unicorn rampant of the earlier version as well as the national plant, a four leafed clover. However, the earlier motto, which had beseeched the Gods for rain, was replaced with a golden sash beneath the shield on which was emblazoned "Veritas Relativa Est" (Truth is Relative). The Chief of Station of the largest donor agency assisted Her Majesty with the unveiling.

* * *

What fun! But certainly no journal editor would publish it, or so I thought. Then a friend steered me toward the Journal of Irreproducible Results (JIR). Published at the University of Chicago, the JIR sets the standard for academic humor. It may be the only edited university journal given over to the genre, which makes it the premier journal in its field. Among its earlier articles was the classic that proved, using solid principles of physics, that bumblebees couldn't fly.

I submitted "The Schweinkopf Hypothesis" for their review. To my amazement, they accepted. Publication followed shortly thereafter. Proudly, but somewhat tongue-in-cheek, I included this publication in my annual performance evaluation report for that year. My department chair was not amused. Nor was my performance rating improved.

I can still hear his gruff response. "Eckert. Why don't you quit playing games and do some serious work for once."

Crestfallen, I retreated, forgot about the Schweinkopf Hypothesis, and moved on to other more "serious work." But not before, on a lark, listing the publication on my résumé. What the heck? I had worked harder on that piece than on most of my other 150 academic publications. It was refereed and published by a well known academic journal at a prestigious university. In my mind it counted. Little did I know that Professor Schweinkopf had not finished with me yet.

Several years later, while working in South Africa, I applied for the job of department head at the prestigious University of Stellenbosch in South African. As part of the screening process, the Dean of Agriculture interviewed me in Pretoria. Almost as soon as we met, he said with a smile that he was pretty sure he was going to hire me.

"Why?" I had expected an extensive grilling.

"Two reasons. For one, you and I were born on the same day. And second, you are the only academic I ever knew who put a JIR article on his résumé." Turns out the dean had a degree from the University of Chicago and knew the JIR very well.

Thank you, Professor Schweinkopf. Thank you two as well, Drs. Quagmire and Mudd. It has been quite a ride. Not only did we publish our "work" together, I also got a job.

A year or two later, Nick Vink, the editor of *Development Southern Africa* (DSA), asked if he might run the "Schweinkopf Hypothesis" in DSA. At that time, DSA was a leading journal carrying the debate on the economic and political future of the region, preparing ground work for all the expected post-apartheid transitions. Nick wanted to have a little fun with his readers. As a result, my fictional professor and his two lovely colleagues frolicked across the pages of the next issue. Same bogus text, now in its second refereed journal.

At that time, the Government of South Africa offered monetary incentives for academics to publish journal articles. Their goal: to stimulate and publicize South African scholarship within the international scientific community. As Department Head, it fell to me to report what my faculty members published each year so that they might receive their individual subsidy awards. DSA was on the list of approved journals. An applicant needed only to submit the title and a first page. THAT first page, the one with all the fifty dollar words. THAT first page which never hinted at the farce to follow. "OK, Professor, and Ladies. One last time, just you and I vs. The System."

That year, the central government subsidy amounted to $800 per article. My virtual friends, the Professor, Chastity, Salome, and I chuckled all the way to the bank to deposit that check.

"Adjust It, Lieutenant"

Dawn, September 8, 1965:   Somewhere over North Vietnam, an American F-105 pilot roars through a morning sky, outrunning his own sound, looking down on monsoon clouds, their tops a sun splashed cotton candy white. He left Thailand an hour ago astride a blowtorch, his 25 tons of fuel and screaming metal splitting the sky with malice. Beneath his wings ride three tons of terror, packaged as 750 pound bombs, each big enough to take out a bridge or crater a highway into disuse. Strapped to his calf is his .45 caliber pistol in case he finds himself standing on unfriendly ground. Another day at the office is underway for the 2nd Air Division.

The F-105, largest single-seat combat aircraft ever built, was designed to carry a single nuclear weapon in its belly, at twice the speed of sound, deep into the Soviet Union. This plane turns with all the grace and dexterity of a supertanker, but it does haul the freight. It is now the workhorse of the air war against North Vietnam. The Air Force calls this plane the Thunderchief. The pilot and his buddies call it the Lead Sled for short, or, with great affection, "Thud," the presumed sound of failing to pull this oversized mechanical marvel up out of a bombing dive. In more than 20,000 combat sorties over Vietnam, 382 F-105s and 62 pilots will be lost before this war is over.

A small problem unfolds for our pilot this morning, one that will grow with time. His strike coordinates lead him out of Thailand, across Laos and into North Vietnam, well north of Hanoi which is exempted by politics from our wrath. When he arrives at target, ground visibility is zero. Most of North Vietnam is weathered in. His assigned target hides somewhere down there beneath two miles of gray sodden monsoon turbulence. He shifts to Plan B, hoping to find a secondary target. F-105s don't return to base with their ordinance. Nobody wants to try landing with all those explosives hanging under their wings just a foot or two off the tarmac. One miscue, one cross draft of breeze, and "thud" would definitely be an understatement. If no secondary targets appear, pilots head home, lighten up by dumping their bombs over unpopulated Laotian jungles, and report their mission as "Canx Wx:" cancelled due to weather.

Today, however, his luck changes up there at 35,000 feet. A hole appears in the clouds, and beneath it, Hot Damn, a railroad bridge spanning a chasm. He doesn't really know where he is, but that sure looks like a secondary target to him. He aligns his Thunderchief with the bridge, dives and cuts loose his load of 750 pounders. Seconds later he grins as flashes walk the length of the bridge, he spits out a satisfied "Gotcha." Now his job becomes getting home in one piece. He claws for altitude. Breaking out above the clouds, off to his right and left, he notes two mountain tops reaching into sunlight. These he circles on the flight map taped to his thigh, marking his strike's location. Back home in Thailand, he's debriefed. His reported "extensive damage" to the bridge, together with the strike's coordinates, are cabled to the 2nd Air Division HQ, at Tan Son Nhut airbase just outside Saigon. There, in the command post, a junior intelligence officer fills out a daily Ops Report, puts it on a clipboard, and hangs it in the press briefing room.

* * *

I once thought I might escape this war. As an Air Force lieutenant with intelligence analysis skills, I had a nice safe desk job in Ohio, spying on the Soviets from a distance. Then someone in Washington decided that we could not afford to lose this war and half a million men and women were dispatched, most of them initially on six months temporary duty. I arrived expecting group barracks with canvas cots, incoming mortars and chow hall grits for breakfast. Instead I got the four-star Majestic Hotel where I learned to love *nuc mam*, Vietnam's famous fermented fish sauce, and eat with chopsticks. I was off duty and sleeping very well that morning while they paid me extra for hazard duty in a war zone.

The command post of the 2nd Air Division lurked behind security doors in a windowless concrete-block building. Inside, it smelled of air conditioner must and dead cigarettes. In chalk on a blackboard running the length of one command post wall, in block letters, stood the Rules of Engagement, mostly bombing guidelines and flight limitations. Here, military and political goals for micro-managing this particular war merged, and not always compatibly. The Rules changed periodically as Washington's politicians systematically varied the war's intensity, attempting to nudge their opponents toward negotiations. The Theory of Limited War which our Defense Department revered at the time, labels this "belligerent communication." The North Vietnamese weren't listening.

The Rules commanded an almost Biblical set of Thou Shalt Nots. With SECRET in capitals at both ends of the blackboard. For example, *Thou Shalt Not*: drop bombs except within 400 yards of a road. Try explaining this to an F-4 Phantom pilot who flies in at 500 mph just above the banana trees to avoid ground fire, then has less than 60 seconds on target to pop up to 5 or 10 thousand feet, find his objective, align his plane, release his ordinance, and get back down among the bananas before a surface-to-air missile locks on and fires. At the speed of sound, a roadway plus or minus 400 yards passes beneath the pilot in less than three seconds. Or, *Thou Shalt Not*: bomb rice paddies, unless . . ., unless fuel, guns or explosives lay hidden in water proof bladders under those paddies, a popular North Vietnamese Army tactic at the time. Find the submerged bladders? In muddy water planted with rice? From 10,000 feet? At Mach 1? If they weren't already bitter, pilots laughed openly. Then there was The Biggie, right at the top of the chalk board. *Thou Shalt Not*: bomb within 30 miles of the Chinese border. The military remembered Korea all too well, and, by God, there would be no Chinese incursion this time around.

My shift at work started about the time that day's Ops report was posted. Later, I would remember one reporter, an intense man, dragging his index finger down the clipboard listing that morning's strikes, pausing on one entry, going to a large wall map of Vietnam, tracing out some coordinates, scratching something in his notebook and quietly, seemingly in haste, leaving the press room. I wondered what was up, but thought nothing more of it at the time.

September 10: The pilot hadn't noticed anything odd. Neither had his debriefing officer. Nor did the lieutenant who compiled and posted the Ops report. However, the award winning reporter from the New York Times saw a pair of coordinates he didn't recognize. When he plotted them out, those mountain tops and that bombed railroad bridge lay only 17 miles from China. Two days elapsed before the Times carried the following on page one:

"By Charles Mohr – Special to the NYT

U.S. Air Strikes Pressed North

. . . United States jets inflicted "extensive" bomb damage Wednesday on a North Vietnamese railroad bridge about 17 miles from the Chinese Communist border."

This little news item seemed nothing more than innocuous reportage from a fluid war. Except that the headline and the seventeen miles raised unacceptable red flags. Washington was pissed. Maybe frightened as well, if Washington can be frightened. This reported violation of the buffer zone surrounding China apparently caught the attention of the President who compulsively micro-managed this war, including personally selecting bombing targets. Scuttlebutt said LBJ was livid.

I was back on duty that night when the red secure phone rang and the major answered. He came to rigid attention which seemed odd in front of a telephone. The circus had just begun. The major handed the call to a bird colonel, who also stiffened. He, in turn, transferred the call to the back room where a brigadier general commanded the night shift. In moments an orderly left the command post at a dead run. Almost immediately he was back with a three-star general loping behind in his pajamas and slippers, his Air Force blue bathrobe flapping in his tailwind. Lt. Gen. Joseph Moore,

Commander, 2nd Air Division, had been asleep in his luxury house trailer just outside the command post. At this moment *his* commander in Washington was calling.

Everyone with eagles on their shoulders locked themselves into the back room. The lieutenants and captains were left sitting there, becalmed in the eye of the storm. Then one of the colonels emerged and strode briskly across to another clipboard on the wall. His index finger traced down the duty roster and stopped at the entry he sought. Turning, he looked at me with all the lethal warmth of one of those 750 pounders. He was probably imagining a terminal crater in my career. Still clueless, I felt a chill nonetheless.

September 11: This afternoon the captains and lieutenants, the paper pushers in the command post, were summoned for a briefing. We gathered in a nervous clot over in one corner right under the Rules of Engagement. A bird colonel told us that a pilot's "mistaken" strike coordinates "implied" that he had bombed too close to China and that this "reporting error" had found its way to the press. The grievousness of this event, if it were true, the potential horror of a Chinese incursion, the political fallout in Washington, all were impressed upon us in command voice. The colonel then instructed those of us handling the intelligence function to ensure that future postings in the press room "complied with the rules of engagement."

"What if a pilot's report doesn't comply?" I asked in my naiveté.

"Adjust it, Lieutenant!" the colonel spat out. He turned on his heel and left.

"Was that a direct order?" I asked my buddy, Captain Moran, with his many more years in the service than I. "You bet," he said. To him it was no big deal. To me, it seemed the press had now become the enemy – and lying to them now official policy. Starting that afternoon, the press received only "sanitized" reports of air combat operations over North Vietnam. "Another day at the office" had just been redefined.

Meanwhile, unknown to those of us in-country, the Washington Post ran this retraction:

"U.S. military authorities said they erred in reporting that U.S. jets bombed a railroad bridge in North Vietnam within 17 miles of Communist China's border . . . planes made their strike about 40 miles from the border . . . error blamed on a mistake in electrical transmission of geographical coordinates."

And then, as if to emphasize the overall sweetness of this air war, the very next paragraph offered:

"U.S. Air Force planes made another toy drop over North Vietnam Thursday, dropping 10,000 packages of soap, school supplies and toys on five population centers. The raid was in observance of Children's Day in Vietnam"

That's right. A "raid." To celebrate Children's Day! I suppose there would have been air raid sirens, bomb shelters frantically sought, and sounds of ack-ack in the distance. And then – toy bombs from your friendly F-105 pilots? I cannot begin to imagine what the average North Vietnamese civilian thought.

September 25: Colonel Rockly Triantafellu commanded intelligence operations for the 2nd Air Division in Vietnam. Ultimately he was my boss. Everyone knew he had been nominated for a star. If confirmed, he would become the first Brigadier General in Air Force intelligence. This was a big deal, even for the junior officers in his command. We were all pulling for him.

Today, however, the crater plopped into my career and a lot of things changed in my view. On arriving at base, I was ordered to report to Col. Triantafellu's office immediately. His assistant, Captain Randall, handed me an ominous military brown envelope, marked, "TO BE OPENED BY ADDRESSEE ONLY." Inside, "Subject: Administrative Admonition" was text to curdle the promotion aspirations of any 1st Lieutenant.

"Your unquestioning acceptance of erroneous intelligence information on 8 September 1965 is a matter of great concern to this command. . . . integrity of required action would have readily revealed the error . . . You are hereby admonished for your derelictions in this matter. Failure to apply . . . professional standards . . . caused numerous man-hours . . . for corrective action." Signed: J.H. Moore, Lieutenant General, USAF, Commander.

"What the Hell is this all about," I muttered. Clueless and shaken, I demanded an explanation. Capt. Randall did his inadequate best. Apparently it had taken the command structure of the 2nd Air Division just two days (*numerous man-hours*) to find a way to convert that F-105 pilot's report into a mistake. Those mountain tops had moved. It had been a cable transmission glitch, that was all. His strike report must have been wrong because it did not comply with the Rules of Engagement. And 1st Lt. Eckert, the lowest ranked officer in the command post, was being admonished for not having had the foresight to sanitize an Ops report, three days *before* sanitizing Ops reports became part of the job. But, why me, I wondered. I had been off duty, sound asleep under the air conditioner in the Majestic Hotel. In his haste, that colonel's accusing finger picked the wrong name off the duty roster, and I became the "derelict" one. Washington was told that "remedial action had been taken." Newspapers reported Air Force spokesmen expressing "embarrassment" over the "reporting error."

My three-page appeal had the audacity to suggest that the pilot's report was correct. We had encroached on China, albeit accidentally. I defended the pilot for doing his best under difficult circumstances. Finding targets is always dicey business in the monsoons. I defended myself by pointing out that we were not ordered to "adjust" Ops reports until later and that, in fact, I wasn't even there that morning. I stamped it all, using Captain Randall's little rubber stamp with the magic words, TOP SECRET, and the red ink. I was about to learn things about the military they never taught me in officers training.

A week later, I inquired of Capt. Randall, "Any progress?"

"He hasn't had time yet," Randall replied. But he made a tactical error when he pulled the file out from the bottom of a wooden in-box. Now I knew where the folder hid and what it looked like. Another week went by. Another visit to Capt. Randall. Same answer. I reached over, fished out my file from the bottom of the in-box and put it on top. "This week for sure? Please. Sir." After another cycle with identical results, I shortened the interval. Every three days or so, I visited the good captain, pulled my file from the bottom of Rockly's in-box, put it on top, expressed my mounting frustration and left. It became our morning routine. My last stop before going off duty, Randall's first vexation as he came to work. We had our little chat and my file cycled, bottom-to-top-to-bottom, probably in less than five minutes. Randall was doing his job. His boss, a WW-II flying ace, was a demigod in Air Force intelligence and he was expecting brigadier's stars. There was just no way in Hell that a little unpleasant nastiness was going to occur on his watch. Not infractions of the Rules of Engagement. And most definitely not buffer zone violations right up under the great rump of China. No Sir! Strike reports were sometimes wrong. Transmission errors happened. And lieutenants were expendable, especially reserve officers on temporary duty, like me, sent over from some stateside desk job, who would soon be gone from the theater anyway. After all, the careers of flight-rated, regular officers were at risk here.

October – November: There was a real war out there in the jungle, but it wasn't much visible from Saigon. In our off duty hours, the junior officers ate French and Vietnamese cuisine, shopped for stereos and ivory carvings, drank 333 export beer in local night clubs and listened to satin voiced Vietnamese women in their Ao Dai national dress sing western country ballads with an accent. On the more memorable nights we would sit in the 6th floor open air bar at the Majestic Hotel and watch the fireworks of Operation Rolling Thunder as B-52s laid their strings of bombs through the distant countryside. Carrying one-hundred-eight 500 pound bombs, a single B-52 left twenty-foot wide craters in a footprint two hundred yards wide and two miles long. And these planes arrived in waves. First came the light from explosions a mile or two away. On top of the Majestic, conversation stopped when the flashes began. Then came the thunder, rolling, for that is really the only term that fits, thunder rolling through the night, leaving a lunar landscape filled with shattered trees and people. Tables rattled – you had to steady your beer. A pulsing sound and light show, air expressed to us nightly from an airbase on Guam. "Waiter, may I have another 333 please? And one for my NBC correspondent buddy here as well.

November 25: FIGMO: Finally, I Got My Orders. I was to leave Vietnam shortly. A wife, a baby daughter and graduate school waited stateside. But so did some small measure of disgrace if I mustered out with General Moore's admonishment still on my record. In desperation, I figured that if politics was driving this war, then I would play that game too. I made one last visit to Captain Randall. We joked about our little game of hide-the-file. I told him I had my orders, but that I really didn't want to leave with a blemished record. I told him that one of my beer drinking buddies there in Saigon was Garrick Uttley, chief of NBC's war correspondents. And then I dropped my own 750 pounder. "Captain. If I don't have a resolution the day before I leave, I will spend my last night in Saigon in the Caravelle Hotel bar with my friends from NBC and CBS. And I'm gonna blow your goddamned idiotic Rules of Engagement all over the front page of every newspaper in the U.S." I turned and walked out. Now there really were some careers on the line. Probably mine. To Hell with it. Let them arrest me if they wanted.

November 26: I arrive for work at Tan Son Nhut airbase with just ten days to go before flying out. Two crisply starched Air Policemen meet me at the gate, their pistols in white plastic holsters hanging on white plastic shoulder straps. Uh Oh, I think. This must be how time in the brig begins. But they seem friendly enough. They invite me for a jeep ride over to the Adjutant General's office. Maybe the brig is over there in a vaulted basement room somewhere, I don't know. So I climb in. At the AG's office I am greeted by a memorable vision of a secretary, the first blond woman in civilian clothes I have seen in six months. She is about six feet tall and gorgeous. "Wouldn't you like some coffee?" she smiles. "And a doughnut? They were just flown in fresh from the States this morning."

In a couple of minutes, a 2-star general emerges, shakes my hand and invites me and my doughnut into his wood paneled office where he hands me a letter. He, also, is smiling. This letter says that I was "not responsible for the derelictions," that I was "admonished without cause," and thanks me for "bringing attention to this matter." It closed with sincere regrets and apologies, all offered on behalf of the same "J.H. Moore, Lieutenant General, USAF, Commander."

Now I knew what really drove the brass to action: the power of this new enemy, the press. The Adjutant General and I each had another imported doughnut and a pleasant chat before I was ushered out. Only later would I recall that those mountain tops remained, according to the Air Force, 40 miles south of China, according to the topo maps, seventeen.

* * *

Just days before his army defeated the French at Dien Bien Phu, Ho Chi Minh made a remarkable proposal to the United States. Secretly, a handful of American military observers had parachuted into Ho's command post. Ho's imminent victory presaged a new national leader and an altered global political matrix. The visitors had been sent by Washington to learn more about this enigmatic man and his movement. They were received graciously and for several days they watched from strategic hilltops as the noose tightened around the encircled French in the valley below. On their last night before departure, they dined with Ho and his top commander, General Vo Nguyen Giap. Not only would Vo defeat the French that month in 1954, two decades later he would command the defeat of the Americans as well. But in 1954, according to the American team leader, an army captain who told me this story, Ho was in an expansive mood. Dinner was roast duck accompanied by a select French red wine with a fine cognac afterward. Toward the end of the evening Ho asked the Americans,

"We have welcomed you, shown you everything you asked to see and answered all your questions. Is there anything else you would like to know?" The captain answered,

"Sir, I have been instructed to ask you one question directly. Are you a communist?" Ho's honest response:

"Yes. But can't our countries still be friends? I want good relations between my Vietnam and your America. Will you take my request to Washington?"

This was 1954. The French surrendered on May 7th. In Washington, Senator Joseph McCarthy was at his crazed zenith, fanning xenophobic flames of anti-communist prejudice and fear. Consequently, America's first really stupid decision on Vietnam was to flatly reject Ho Chi Minh's earnest request. At the time, America viewed communism through the paranoiac lens of Eisenhower's "Domino Theory" with its apocalyptic Orwellian outcomes. Thus blinded, we shoved Vietnam further beyond any rational consideration, another exercise in mass stupidity. Finally, once we had troops on the ground, the peculiarly Theory of Limited War, with its fatal, built-in psychological errors, drove the war's strategy. In a nutshell, we prosecuted a war against a nation that sought our friendship, driven to fight almost "at all costs" by anti-communist paranoia, using a military theory that could not possibly succeed.

In the end, well over two million Vietnamese died. To us they were easily destroyed because they were nameless, dehumanized with faceless epithets; Charlie, gooks and others. They are now only ciphers in the history books. B-52 bombing, for all its might and majesty, was little more than a high-tech but basically blind, scorched-earth tactic of incredible cost. Historians say Operation Rolling Thunder killed 180,000 civilians as well as a few combatants. More than 58,000 Americans gave their all to this ill begotten war, leaving behind dark chasms in the lives of their loved ones. Another 300,000 came home wounded, a quarter of them losing a limb. 9,000 took their own lives afterward. For these Americans, all that ends did not end well. Somewhere in Thailand, an F-105 pilot was court martialed, or so Captain Randall told me. For him the war did not end well either. I imagine he drove a desk for the rest of his truncated Air Force career.

There was other news as well. After September 11th, all aerial operations over North Vietnam were in full compliance with the Rules of Engagement. Charlie Mohr, whose accurate report on September 10th precipitated years of official lies, "became one of a handful of correspondents whose reporting challenged false official accounts and presaged the failure of American and Vietnamese policies in the war" according to a New York Times' tribute published at his death in 1989. In an ironic twist, Mohr was decorated *by our army*, receiving a

Bronze Star for heroism he showed trying to rescue a dying soldier while wounded himself. The Colonel? He became Brigadier General Rockly Triantafellu on November 1, 1965, proceeded on to his second star, and completed his distinguished career with a lofty assignment in the Pentagon. And me? I left the madness to those for whom it was a profession. I flew home to my family, an honorable discharge and a career in international *non-military* service. The Air Force sent me off with memories and souvenirs; a commendation medal for "distinctive achievement," a Vietnam service medal and an outstanding unit award for "exceptionally meritorious service under combat conditions." So we in the 2nd Air Division must have done something right. Or did we?

Author's Note: *That campfire in Namibia which spawned the Namib Roots story above sent my mind in several directions. This story starts at the same campfire yet follows a different trajectory. I hope the reader will forgive a couple of paragraphs that I duplicated in the interests of telling this story fully.*

Requiem for the Night Sky

Flames from desert-dried acacia wood pushed back the night, enfolding those of us there on the sand in succulent warmth. Flaming coals quivered orange and blue. This fire whispered softly, exhaling resins trapped long years ago. A strenuous day hunting in the Namibian sun and wind had left my body drained. The hunt now over, my friend Helmut, the game ranch owner, and a few of his closer friends reclined around this campfire under a towering camel thorn tree. I watched their bonds renew by firelight, bonds so vital when friends live scores of miles apart across an unforgiving desert. We spoke softly of antelope and leopards, cattle and grass, recalled hunts of prior years, and in this sere yet somehow nourishing land, we talked of rain. Spirits of Khoisan Bushmen, a part of this landscape for unnumbered millennia, seemed to swirl around us. They would have also gathered around family fires beneath camel thorn trees, their click-tongued language softened by kinship and a fire's warmth. And they, too, would have talked of rain, the metronome of desert life. A night bird passing overhead might have seen our fire, its glow, our little circle of friends as an orange nipple on the vast black breast of Africa.

Conversations in German eddied around me; my tired mind struggled to keep up. I needed to get up and move, to shake out the kinks, to breathe some cooler air or else succumb to lethargy and sleep. From upwind, a jackal's scent drifted across our group. Wild desert lay just beyond the firelight. Stiffly, I rose from the sand, turned my back to the fire, and walked away. Sharp, late fall air stung my cheeks. It would freeze before dawn. Warmth leaked from my jacket. The chill dragged me from my stupor, into the brilliance of a savannah night on the edge of the Great Namib Desert. My feet found ruts – an old ranch road leading out into the thorn bush – and I followed them, mostly by feel.

As I meandered along the ruts and away from the fire's glow, a living savannah emerged from darkness. Forms of gray and shadows replaced the black. Then came more subtle shades. Some leaves, the waxy ones, winked back at me in lighter grays while others quivered in the breeze, just silhouettes. Something small, but darker than the sand around it, scuttled away from the track into taller grasses. Now with retinas fully bathed in visual purple, my eyes replaced my toes at searching out the path.

Above, the sky radiated points of white fire. So many flickering stars – it seemed as if the whole sky were alive and dancing. The Khoisan drew creation myths from among those stars, from that giant arch of light. But the constellations up there, those they might have named, were lost to me among a million gleaming pinpoints. I wandered through that crystalline night stunned with the enormity of the southern sky, alone with my insignificance. And I found the creation story I that had come to understand, anchored and shaped anew by the mysteries of that teeming firmament overhead.

I watched the night sky a lot after that. Back home in Colorado, we moved to a farm ten miles outside Fort Collins. My cigarette breaks took me out into the night every hour or so for years until I quit that lethal habit. Lunar phases became my metronome, marking off the seasons in 29.5-day intervals. I timed my hunts, my camping trips, by whether I wanted a full moon or darkness after sunset. One year, I watched a rare event, twin dog stars chasing the moon for a couple of nights. As I did, I recalled the Apache legend, so parallel to the Christian story. They say the Moon as virgin goddess mated with an omnipotent Sun-god, and conceived the Dog Star as their precious offspring. Another native people had found a divinity among the stars.

Then came View Point, a clot of tract homes just across the road from our farm, planted five to the acre, all uniformly painted in neutral grays and fenced so they needn't view each other's back yards filled with dog poop and plastic children's gyms. My hayfield of luxuriant, hip-high Brome grass, with voles and hawks and bull snakes and a resident momma fox, gave that cookie-cutter subdivision its ironic name. I planted 40 Austrian pines up by the house to screen them out. That should have been enough. However, someone felt they needed street lights over there and someone else decided they could save some money by not shielding them. When they finished, I could count, from my front door, 52 mercury-vapor, 300-watt bulbs glowing down, and out, and up. Although View Point lay half a mile away, I could almost read a newspaper at night using View Point's public lighting. Above these glaring blots, my eastern sky disappeared, replaced by a sickly orange glowing. The moon got through. Jupiter also made it. But Mars struggled. Most of everything else, if it lay to the east, is now only a suggestion or a memory.

As we lose our darkest skies, we have finally come to value them. But rather like endangered species, only when they face extinction do we gather the force of public will and pool our treasure to protect them. Even then, most likely it will not be enough, nor in time. Those who care rail against the creep of "skyglow," that dome of light seen ever more frequently over cities, rural shopping centers, sports stadia and elsewhere. Their rallying cry has become Dark Skies!, their efforts given focus through The International Dark-Sky Association, (http://www.darksky.org).

The unfathomed night sky first captured a part of me on a family camping trip in early August 1953, some 16 years before our moon landing gave everyone a new celestial perspective. In those days, camping with Dad meant hauling a trailer full of mattresses out into the Arizona desert, laying them on tarps between the cacti, and cooking hot dogs, refried beans and stick bread over a mesquite fire while coyotes sang in the distance. As we snuggled into our blankets, the Perseid meteor shower exploded across the heavens. I'd never seen anything like it and I couldn't sleep. Next day, the newspaper called it the most intense shower of the 20th century. For hours, it seemed, I watched, entranced as the sky fired tracer bullets. I must have slept at some point because I woke around 2 a.m. looking up from my mattress at the underside of a curious javelina's snout. For a split second, I saw a bristled nose twitching, and some short razor tusks. Then I moved, recoiled perhaps, because my startled visitor exploded through the middle of camp, knocking over our cooking gear. "What the heck was that," came from Dad's mattress. Perseus, the first of the Twelve Olympians of ancient Greek mythology, still blazed away, once or twice a minute.

About this time, Boy Scouting taught me the major constellations of the northern sky and some basics of celestial

264

navigation. The Big and Little Dippers led to Polaris in the north just as surely as the sun rose in the east and moss grew mostly on the northern side of pine trees. Knowing these and a few other pointers, we could never get lost in the woods. And if we could navigate the wilderness, why not life's trickier pathways as well? Scouting's biggest lesson, "Be Prepared."

My 1948 Boy Scout Handbook taught only the barest rudiments of navigating by the stars. Certainly the Spanish, the Portuguese or the Vikings had a vastly more complex knowledge of the heavens under which they sailed. But then, they also had an unadulterated night sky to guide them. Today we build our telescopes on the highest mountains, or in underdeveloped countries, or we send them into space to escape our artificial lights, the lumen waste of living.

Just how much natural light is out there in those dark skies? The answer depends on what we mean by "light." Interstellar dust and detritus block out much of the visible spectrum. Light that does reach us has often bounced around the universe, diffused by impacts, bent by gravity, or refracted through spatial aerosols. It arrives as a background haze, as glows and glimmers of different hues, or other subtle differences from a jet-black nothingness. However, when I see a star, its bright pinpoint fixed at some celestial coordinates, I know that bit of light came straight through the entire maze, unobstructed. There is a special bond between us, in a way, to know that my retina is the first opaque substance that tiny shaft of starlight has found in the millions of years and miles of its journey. It will also be the last. That glimmer is mine alone.

Even before the stars finally slip behind pollution's curtain, more subtle cosmic lights will long be gone. Besides the stars, other lights we see at night form a rare brotherhood. "Airglow," for instance, keeps the night sky from ever being completely dark. Scores of miles above the Earth, the sky teems with cosmic rays tearing through the upper atmosphere, knocking molecules apart, leaving surplus bits adrift as fractions of their former selves. The energy released by all these ions and electrons as they find new homes, reuniting with others of their kind, appears to us as light; yellow-hued for oxygen ions or blue for nitrogen.

"Zodiacal light" arrives on the bounce. Sunlight ricochets off interplanetary clouds of cosmic dust, reaching us in much the same spectrum as it left its source, but dulled and diffused by whatever light the dust absorbed. It doesn't take much dust to bounce this light our way. Single particles, just one millimeter in diameter, scattered every 8 kilometers throughout space, would produce our zodiacal light. It must be dusty up there. Zodiacal light is more than half the total light that reaches us on a moonless night.

"Gegenschein," literally "shines against," is a special case. Gegenschein also bounces off of cosmic dust, but not with a glancing blow. These dust motes lie on the other side of the earth, directly opposite the sun. The sun's rays hit them in full phase before bouncing back for our delight. Just as the light from a full moon outshines other lunar phases, Gegenschein is zodiacal light at its brightest. We see it as a hazy, softly lit circle moving across the moonless sky.

"Auroral light" draws its power from the solar wind. Incoming charged particles are snagged by earth's magnetic field which sucks them in, spiraling down along magnetic field lines. Collisions in our upper atmosphere excite these electrons causing quantum leaps from one state to another.

Then, reverting to their former state, they lose their kinetic energy gained in those collisions and it becomes shimmering light. Greens and red arise from oxygen, a pink or blue-violet tinge from nitrogen. On rare occasions, atmospheric neon throws out a waving orange curtain with rippled edges. Is it any wonder that the Cree people call the Aurora Borealis the "Dance of the Spirits?"

* * *

Vexed with the imprecision of the dark sky dialogue, the astronomer John Bortle created the Bortle Dark Sky Scale in 2001, calling attention to the growing threat of light pollution. He defined nine classes, ranging from Class 1 - "Excellent Dark Sky Site" to Class 9 - "Inner City Sky." In Class 1, zodiacal light and gegenschein are both visible. Airglow is readily apparent. He rejoices, *"If you are observing on a grass-covered field bordered by trees, your telescope, companions, and vehicle are almost totally invisible. This is an observer's Nirvana!"*

Bortle's Class 9 is a frightening portent of where we are likely headed as a civilization. His definition speaks of loss: *"The entire sky is brightly lit, even at the zenith. Many stars making up familiar constellation figures are invisible, and dim constellations like Cancer and Pisces are not seen at all. - - - The only celestial objects that really provide pleasing telescopic views are the Moon, the planets, and a few of the brightest star clusters (if you can find them)."*

Responding to public awareness of our vanishing dark skies, the National Park Service recently surveyed the night sky in all our parks and monuments. Natural Bridges National Monument in Utah emerged the winner, scoring 2 on the

Bortle Scale. The Park Service then bestowed the name, "The World's First International Dark Sky Park." I camped there during the dark of the moon in March 2009. Just as in Namibia, I took an hour's walk at midnight. And as in Namibia, the constellations were lost within the brilliant scatter overhead. Again, I was struck dumb by the enormity of it all; by the mysteries of the sky's inner workings driven by cosmic laws so far beyond my comprehension.

But I wonder. Like an old Siberian tiger pacing out his final years in a Russian zoo, we may have already lost something forever when we have to put it on display. The title "World's First International Dark Sky Park" is perhaps more lament than honor.

As we lose when our night sky, when Polaris slips from view, it's more than just a Boy Scout memory flickering out. Polaris is one constant in our life, a tent peg in the firmament, a welcome friend that anchors travels through our darkness. Thus directed, we find a sense of self assurance, and find ourselves within the landscape. Without Orion, young boys won't dream so easily of slaying beasts, and in that dream find an inner strength to face their monsters. When we have mapped the last piece of *terra incognita*, turned the seabed into a commodity, and waved a final farewell to Orion and Cassiopeia, king and queen of the night sky, we will have lost more than just the view. If we never stand, wide eyes cast upward, awed by the incalculable vastness out there, we are unlikely to sense what minuscule motes we really are. And if we can't, will we then conclude our universe is bounded by a skyglow dome, and leap to the arrogant presumption that we control it all? If we do, we will then have truly lost our way.

Glossary

Names, Places and Other Terms

ANC - The African National Congress, the mostly black political party of Nelson Mandela which has governed the country since the first democratic election.

CIMMYT - Universally used acronym for the International Center for Maize and Wheat Improvement Center (in Spanish, Centro Internacional de Majoramiento de Maiz y Trigo). CIMMYT grew from a research program begun in Mexico in the 1940s by the Rockefeller Foundation, became the first of the International Agricultural Research Centers (IARCs) and subsequently part of the Consultative Group on International Agricultural Research (CGIAR).

Coloured - A racial category established by South Africa's white parliament many years ago as a segregation tool. Includes all people of mixed race, plus the ethnically distinct Bushmen. Excluded are whites, blacks and persons of Indian descent, each of which were treated separately in national statistics.

CSU - Colorado State University

Expat - Short for expatriate. A person living outside his or her country of citizenship. Refers to diplomatic and foreign assistance personnel overseas. Derived from the verb "to expatriate" referring to a nation removing one's citizenship, usually by a legal process.

Khotso Ntate - "Peace, Father" in Sesotho. The traditional greeting of the Basotho people.

LASA - The Lesotho Agricultural Sector Analysis project. A team of six Colorado State University specialists posted in Maseru, Lesotho from August 1977 to August 1980, working mostly in the Planning Division of the Ministry of Agriculture.

Marshall Plan - A massive program of U.S. assistance to rebuild Europe after WWII. Named after President Truman's Secretary of State, George Marshall, this program lasted four years from April 1948 onward. $13 billion was invested, or approximately $127 Billion in 2014 dollars.

Maseru - Capital city of Lesotho and the seat of national government.

Mission, The - Short name for a USAID Mission to a country, the official offices of USAID.

Neem tree - *Azadirachta indica*, a member of the mahogany family native to India, Pakistan and elsewhere in South Asia. Tolerates drought and brackish water well, produces air borne chemicals famous for repelling mosquitoes.

North-West Frontier Province (NWFP) - A collection of smaller districts of Pakistan, north and west of Punjab Province, lying along the border with Afghanistan. Populated by the Pathan tribe, this region has, until recently, fallen largely outside the control or influence of the Pakistani government.

South-West Africa - As German South-West Africa this huge expanse of arid land was a German colony from 1884 to 1915. It became a trustee of South Africa after WWI under a League of Nations mandate. Independence came in on March 21, 1990. Now Namibia, the nation includes much of the Kalahari and Great Namib deserts.

Sotho - Many stories herein deal with the Southern Sotho people of southern Africa. The term "Sotho," pronounced *soo too*, forms the base of several nouns.

Lesotho - The country, approximately the size of the state of Maryland. Lesotho (*lay soo too*) lies fully inside South Africa. Since all of Lesotho is 5,000 feet above sea level, its nickname is The Mountain Kingdom. In 1868, Great Britain made the country a protectorate of the crown, along with areas that are now Botswana and Swaziland thus protecting them from absorption by South Africa. Lesotho received its independence in 1966.

Mosotho - An individual of Sotho ethnicity, singular.

Basotho - Individuals of Sotho ethnicity, plural
Sesotho - (*say soo too*) The language of the Basotho people.

Third World - Originally referring to the group of non-aligned nations which attempted to remain neutral in the

East-West tussles of the Cold War. More commonly used in later years to imply all under developed or lesser developed nations.

USAID - United States Agency for International Development, the branch of America's Department of State responsible for our non-military foreign assistance program. Their offices and personnel in Washington D.C. are called AID to distinguish from field branches.

West Pakistan - At independence from India in 1947, the Muslim dominated areas became part of the new state of Pakistan. The Indian state of Bengal became East Pakistan while the other four provinces of Punjab, Sind, Baluchistan and the NWFP constituted West Pakistan. After the 1971 war with India, East Pakistan became Bangladesh and West Pakistan became simply Pakistan.

Author's Resume

1939-41   Born to Phil and Eva Eckert, both parents from Ohio dairy farms. Baby years in Ohio.

1941-42   First international year in Mexico City.

1942-46   Childhood in Cleveland OH and Bozeman MT.

1946-47   Second grade in Turrialba, Costa Rica attending one-room school in the jungle.

1947-48   Bozeman, MT again.

1948-50   Fourth and fifth grades at American Community School, Paris France.

1950-51   Sixth grade in Arlington, VA.

1951-55   Seventh through tenth grades in Tucson, AZ.

1955-57   Last two years of high school in Germany, at home in Bonn, at school in Frankfurt.

1957-59   University Student at the University of Arizona, majored in agricultural economics.

1959-60   Year of study abroad at University of Bonn, concentrated on agricultural policy and the emerging Common Market, the predecessor to the European Union.

1960-62   B.Sc. at the University of Arizona, commissioned via ROTC into USAF.

1962-62   MA degree in development economics at Food Research Institute, Stanford.

1963-65   First Lieutenant, USAF. Intelligence officer at Wright-Patterson AFB in Ohio for two years, then in Vietnam for last half of 1965.

1966-67 Doctoral candidate in agricultural development economics at Michigan State University, East Lansing. Ph.D. awarded 1970 based on research in Pakistan.

1968-71 Employed by Ford Foundation as agricultural policy advisor to the Government of West Pakistan. Based in Lahore, worked throughout the country.

1972-75 Employed by Colorado State University (CSU) as agricultural economist on USAID-funded Pakistan On-Farm Water Management Research Project. Based in Islamabad, worked throughout the country.

1975-77 Assoc. Professor, agricultural economics, CSU, Fort Collins, CO.

1977-80 Chief of Party, Lesotho Agricultural Sector Analysis (LASA) project, in Maseru.

1981-87 Principle Investigator, Income Distribution, Employment and Regional Development in South Africa project. One-third time, worked in Prime Minister's offices, Pretoria.

1981-86 Project Director, USAID funded Gambian Mixed Farming and Resource Management project. One-third time, directed project from CSU campus.

1987-90 Directed development projects with Navajo Nation in Window Rock, AZ and with resource-poor Hispanic farmers in Colorado's San Luis Valley. Directed Institution for Income Distribution and Development Studies on CSU campus.

1991 Fulbright Professor, School of Economics, University of Cape Town, South Africa.

1992-95 Senior Policy Analyst and Research Fellow, Development Bank of Southern Africa.

1993-95 Simultaneously employed as Professor and Department Head, Department of Agricultural Economics, University of Stellenbosch, in South Africa.

1996-06 Professor of Agricultural Development Economics, CSU, Fort Collins, CO, retired 6/06.

2007   Nonfiction writer, based in Vail, AZ and Fort Collins, CO

Previously Published

Several chapters have been previously published with slightly different edits as follows:

"Mahlapane's Story," appeared in *The Superstition Review*, No. 5 (Spring 2010), and also won Northern Colorado Writers 2011 nonfiction essay contest.

"Last Shot," appeared in *Pilgrimage*, Vol. 35, Issue 2, (Fall 2010).

"Evening Hymn," appeared in *Matter 14: Animals*, (December 2011).

"Ismail," appeared in *Memoir Journal*, No. 10 (Fall 2012).

"The Dustbin Telegraph," appeared in *The Superstition Review*, No. 9 (April 2012).

"Adjust it Lieutenant" appeared as "Truth and Consequences," *Pilgrimage*, (Summer 2008).

"Requiem for the Night Sky," appeared in *Weber – The Contemporary West*, (Fall 2012), also awarded the 2012 O. Marvin Lewis Essay Award

About Jerry

Jerry was a professor of agricultural economics at Colorado State University which sent him to live more than 20 years on projects in South Asia and southern Africa. As an academic, he wrote nearly 200 articles and professional papers, two of which won Best Published Article awards. His work redirected agricultural and labor policies in Pakistan and Lesotho and contributed to food grain self-sufficiency in Pakistan and Gambia. In South Africa his research and writing spurred the White government to accelerate abandoning apartheid by creating a Black middle class. He also wrote the basic treatise which framed much of an interracial dialogue on rights in South Africa leading, ultimately, to a new Bill of Rights in the 1997. Several op-eds in the Christian Science Monitor influenced American policy toward South Africa. He ended his overseas career by writing the first economic strategies for the incoming Mandela government.

Jerry's early nonfiction celebrated the natural world, especially wildlife, in American and Pakistani outdoor magazines. He wrote a hunting and fishing column in the Fort Collins Coloradoan for two years. Following retirement, his literary nonfiction appeared in *Pilgrimage, Matter, The Superstition Review, Weber: The Contemporary West, Memoir Journal, Ruminate*, and elsewhere. "Mahlapane's Story," first published in *The Superstition Review*, won the Northern Colorado Writers 2011 essay competition.

Walk away quietly in any direction and taste the freedom of the mountaineer. Camp out among the grasses and gentians of glacial meadows, in craggy garden nooks full of nature's darlings. Climb the mountains and get their good tidings, Nature's peace will flow into you as sunshine flows into trees. The winds will blow their own freshness into you and the storms their energy, while cares will drop off like autumn leaves.

~John Muir

Jerry Eckert (1939-2015)